Additional Praise for Howard
and
Where's My Fifteen Minutes?

"While [I was] preparing for a very difficult speech, Howard Bragman helped me to communicate more clearly, understand the nature of public discourse, and get my message across. I'm grateful for his wise counsel."

—RON MEYER, PRESIDENT AND COO, UNIVERSAL STUDIOS

"When I was attacked in the press by two jealous troublemakers, Howard Bragman called and kindly offered to help. His phone call was a godsend. If you have Howard on your team, you're in luck."

—GEORGE CHRISTY, JOURNALIST AND SOCIETY COLUMNIST

"Professor Bragman gave me a better understanding of the media at a time when I was overwhelmed by the frenzy. He cleared a foggy perspective I had of the media by digging deep into his many years of experience."

—CARSON PALMER, FORMER USC STUDENT OF HOWARD
BRAGMAN'S, 2002 HEISMAN TROPHY WINNER

"Howard Bragman may be Hollywood's most effective publicity professional. He's clear-eyed, cool-headed, good-humored, and creative. No one can do what Bragman does, but now everyone can see how he does it."

—CHARLES FLEMING, ENTERTAINMENT JOURNALIST AND AUTHOR

"Howard Bragman is the rare public relations practitioner who blends innate communication skills with a deep knowledge of corporate America and an intricate understanding of the entertainment industry. A publicist extraordinaire, Howard knows how to both bring a story to life and kill the story before it becomes a crisis."

—LARRY WEBER, PR VISIONARY

"Our struggle for equality will succeed because an orchestra of strong voices worked together, educating and advocating every step of the way. One of those voices belongs to Howard Bragman, a smart and generous man whose contributions have been a catalyst in changing attitudes and perceptions of lesbians and gay men in America."
—JOAN M. GARRY, FORMER EXECUTIVE DIRECTOR, GAY & LESBIAN ALLIANCE AGAINST DEFAMATION (GLAAD)

"Howard Bragman's advice was an enormous help for our family in coping with the media frenzy during our involvement in the Clinton political debacle."
—DR. BERNARD S. LEWINSKY, FATHER OF MONICA LEWINSKY

"Howard Bragman is all about sheer honesty and unprecedented humor in a field way too full of phonies. Like no publicity artist alive whom I've encountered (and there have been more than I'd care to recall), Howard has always told me the truth."
—BILL ZEHME, JOURNALIST AND AUTHOR

"I love Howard Bragman and his advice because of his heart, his vision, and his courage."
—ISAIAH WASHINGTON, ACTOR

WHERE'S MY FIFTEEN MINUTES?

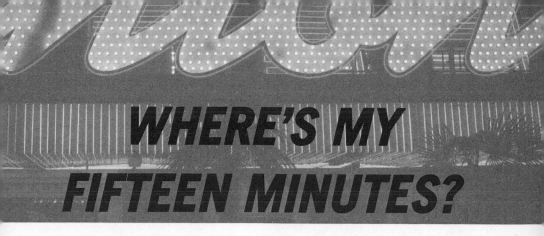

WHERE'S MY FIFTEEN MINUTES?

Get Your Company, Your Cause, or Yourself the Recognition You Deserve

HOWARD BRAGMAN
WITH MICHAEL LEVIN

PORTFOLIO

PORTFOLIO

Published by the Penguin Group
Penguin Group (USA) Inc., 375 Hudson Street,
New York, New York 10014, U.S.A.
Penguin Group (Canada), 90 Eglinton Avenue East, Suite 700,
Toronto, Ontario, Canada M4P 2Y3
(a division of Pearson Penguin Canada Inc.)
Penguin Books Ltd, 80 Strand, London WC2R 0RL, England
Penguin Ireland, 25 St. Stephen's Green, Dublin 2, Ireland
(a division of Penguin Books Ltd)
Penguin Books Australia Ltd, 250 Camberwell Road, Camberwell,
Victoria 3124, Australia
(a division of Pearson Australia Group Pty Ltd)
Penguin Books India Pvt Ltd, 11 Community Centre, Panchsheel Park,
New Delhi—110 017, India
Penguin Group (NZ), 67 Apollo Drive, Rosedale, North Shore 0632,
New Zealand (a division of Pearson New Zealand Ltd)
Penguin Books (South Africa) (Pty) Ltd, 24 Sturdee Avenue,
Rosebank, Johannesburg 2196, South Africa

Penguin Books Ltd, Registered Offices:
80 Strand, London WC2R 0RL, England

First published in 2008 by Portfolio,
a member of Penguin Group (USA) Inc.

10   9   8   7   6   5   4   3   2   1

LIBRARY OF CONGRESS CATALOGING IN PUBLICATION DATA
Bragman, Howard.
    Where's my fifteen minutes? : get your company, your cause or yourself the
recognition you deserve / Howard Bragman with Michael Levin.
        p.   cm
    Includes index.
    ISBN 978-1-59184-236-1
    1.   Public relations.   2.   Publicity.   I. Levin, Michael Graubart.   II.   Title.
    HD59.B726 2008
    659.2—dc22

                                                                2008042120

Printed in the United States of America
Set in ITC Legacy Serif
Designed by Sabrina Bowers

FOR CHUCK

CONTENTS

FOREWORD

☆ BY LEEZA GIBBONS

It's been said that everything you do or say is public relations. And everyone needs good public relations these days, not just the celebrities I've interviewed over the years. The truth is, with today's 24/7 news cycles and the potential for instant Internet phenoms, fame has extended well beyond TV and movie stars. The spotlight can fall on anyone, at any time—from indicted CEOs, politicians, athletes, people in sects, criminals, and cardinals, to everyday people who achieve something extraordinary, or just happen to be in the right place at the right time. What you do when the spotlight falls on you can determine whether you'll be famous, infamous, or immediately fade back into obscurity.

Like it or not, we all need to know how to manage our own public relations. And that's why Howard Bragman is a good friend to have. I've known Howard for more than twenty of the thirty years he's been working in PR. Despite his long career, he represents a new generation of PR experts, and has become the go-to guy in the entertainment industry for crisis management. After thirty years, he has a deep understanding of what any crisis or misstep can mean for a celebrity's career, and vast practical knowledge of what they can do to fix it. Simply put, Howard is the best in the business. When the situation is especially challenging, Howard knows how to handle it. When news breaks, every media outlet wants his opinion, myself included.

So what can Howard do for you? Maybe you picked up this book because you dream of celebrity and fame, of walking down the red carpet and being swamped by crowds of reporters. Perhaps you're trying to figure out how to get people to pay attention to the wonderful things your company or organization is accomplishing. Or maybe, like me, you want to turn the spotlight on a cause that's important to you and could benefit from much more positive attention. Whatever your goal, Howard is your guy. He can show you, step by step, how to make the most of your personal marketability and get the attention you deserve.

Howard is also a natural storyteller. His book is full of stories—real-life examples of PR success stories and crises from Howard's considerable career. From these stories, he creates a practical guide to the proper employment of spin. This is something we all need. Whoever we are—whether we're aiming for the big screen or local attention, business success or a successful bake sale—we all have our fifteen minutes. Whether you can make yours last is up to you, but Howard's advice will certainly help. This missive is a must-read for anyone who seeks or falls into the limelight.

WHERE'S MY FIFTEEN MINUTES?

CHAPTER 1

WHERE'S MY FIFTEEN MINUTES?

Andy Warhol saw it coming. More than forty years ago the iconic artist and philosopher predicted a world in which "everyone will be famous for fifteen minutes." Guess what? That future is now.

Never before have reputations been created and lost so quickly. Never before has an "average Joe" had such a chance to reach the heights and depths in so record a time, and on such a public stage.

We're attracted to attention like moths to a flame. We see how it can boost careers, make people millions of dollars, and seemingly make dreams come true. But, like the moth, the closer we get to the flame, the greater the chance that we may get burned.

Publicity, fame, attention, recognition—these are powerful tools. In my thirty-plus years of working in the public relations and communications worlds, I have seen the good it can do. I have helped people get their messages out. Some have made amazing career advances; many have built smart, profitable businesses; others have changed the world by calling attention to wrongs, curing diseases, or teaching the world to be more accepting of our differences.

But I have seen the other side too. I have helped people burdened with unspeakable woes. Some have been tarnished by scandals of worldwide proportions; others have been victims of crimes and heinous acts; still others have uttered a wrong word in a heated moment and become poster children for bad behavior. Some have made mistakes and been caught; for others, accusations, true or otherwise, have put them through unbelievable pain and sorrow.

The circumstances were different in every situation. Yet, in virtually every case, the right communications made the situation better, if not perfect. For those trying to better themselves, PR was able to facilitate their ascension. It got their messages out cheaper, better, faster, more efficiently, and, hopefully, without backlash. And for those in pain, I tried to lessen their public humiliation, control the damage, and get them back on their feet more quickly so they could continue on with their lives and careers.

Some have compared the effects of PR to lubrication in a machine. I can tell you that it's even more important than that. Life is not a machine; it's an organic, changing organism, and communications and messages are like lifeblood in the system. They nourish, transport, and even sustain health. Everyone won't be famous. But more people than ever before will become public figures. And I promise you, ordinary people do become famous as an ironic by-product of time and circumstance—even in cases in which they might not want it.

Further, everyone has a reputation, an image—people who look to them and judge them. That's just the nature of the world we live in. If you're reading this book, you probably instinctively understand that there is power and pull to life in the public eye: life at a higher level; the chance to influence and lead more people; and perhaps most important, the opportunity to make the world a better place and to make your own life better, happier, and more productive.

At the same time, there are dramatic changes taking place in the way the world communicates. Things like Web sites, You-Tube.com, MySpace.com, Facebook.com, blogs, and iPhones weren't even in our orbit a decade ago and now, for many of us, they are our primary avenues for acquiring and disseminating information and entertainment. The speed, scope, and power of the "new media" are simply staggering. Even a seasoned communications professional like me has had to make dramatic and sometimes uncomfortable changes in my professional and personal life to accommodate them. It's no wonder that the inexperienced person can be so intimidated by the communications superhighway ahead. Should you? Would you? Could you begin to cultivate an image for yourself, your business, or your passion? This book will help you answer those questions.

I'm here to help. This book is not going to make you famous overnight or solve all your communications problems, should you have any. But it will offer insight into the way it works out there in the real world, in the trenches. I'll offer the good news and the bad. I'll be honest, share some of my experiences, try to make them relevant for you, and teach you how to think about communications and look at it in a new and different way. What I do is part art and part science. I have made mistakes, as I will point out in the chapters ahead. But I have certainly had a lot of clients and an amazing array of experiences over the years and far more successes than failures. If nothing else, I'm tough to impress and even tougher to frighten with most communications situations.

I truly believe in an informed, intelligent society. I believe it's time to open the curtain so others can begin to define themselves, change the world, or just simply communicate better and clearer in a crowded and noisy world. You can take what I say with a grain of salt—after all, I've got a point of view. It may not be the same as yours or even as others' in my profession. But I would be surprised if even the most experienced and cynical among you couldn't learn at least a few things from my decades of experience.

We all know that the media move very quickly. In my world, I try to slow things down at least a bit—to take a beat, a deep breath, and really focus on the big picture; to take the pulse and inject a little humanity and empathy into the situation. My belief is that it's not always how fast you do something, it's how well you do it. At the same time, I am not a reductionist. Every idea in the world cannot be turned into a sound bite. All sides of an argument are not morally equal. Sometimes people need the opportunity to express complicated ideas. I have made that happen.

I love to mentor. Whether it was the college students I have taught, my associates, clients, or the media—the chance to offer insight and guidance is a gift. There's far too little mentoring in this world. Let me mentor you.

Your responsibilities include being open to different points of view, to exploring compelling ideas on your own, and to accepting the truths that work for you and rejecting those that don't. If we do it that way, we're going to have a good time and learn something along the way. That will make me feel good and you even smarter. What more could we ask for?

Let me give you a little history lesson. In the past, if you had an important message to get out to consumers, voters, or the community at large, you advertised—either on TV or in newspapers or on the radio. There are two problems with that approach today. First, fewer and fewer people pay attention to traditional media. Everybody's on the Internet—watching videos on their mobile devices, instant messaging, or just hanging out. Young people in particular watch very little over-the-air TV, especially when compared with a generation ago. One major ad agency shared a statistic with me that says it all: in 1985, it took five television commercials to reach 85 percent penetration of the TV-viewing households; in 2008, it took 1,292 commercials to achieve the same penetration.

The other problem with relying on advertising is that it's hard to get people to pay attention to it—or to believe it. It's more difficult than ever to "cut through the clutter" of television, radio, newspapers, and even Internet advertising. People just tune it out. And when they *are* paying attention, it's a challenge to get them to believe the message. Consumers are cynical, jaded, and bored with advertising—and rightly so. At the same time, we are gullible. Gullible and cynical is a very dangerous combination. Remember the story that ran rampant on the Internet about Paris Hilton helping drunken elephants? Even the Associated Press spread it, but no one checked with Ms. Hilton to see if it was true. And how about the time our own government, in the guise of FEMA, hosted a fake news conference—complete with fake journalists and fake questions? And, contrary to an Internet rumor that spread like wildfire, Will Smith does not respect Adolf Hitler and he won a lawsuit saying just that.

Proof that advertising is losing some of its power can be gleaned from the fact that the Super Bowl, the biggest TV event of the year, is watched by fewer than 100 million people. One hundred million sounds like a big number . . . until you consider the fact that more than 200 million Americans have figured out something else to do with their time than sit around and watch a game that, more often than not, lacks suspense. Yes, many people tune in just to see the ads, but those ads are more for shock value or winning awards than actually getting people to buy things. Super Bowl ads are also available online immediately, along with an instant analysis of them, numerous unused versions, and voting on which are the best. The Super Bowl has so many ads that it's just one more location for advertising clutter—and now most of the ads are used to draw people to the Internet. The ads that garner the most success are often the ones that have the best marketing campaigns behind them and that resonate with an existing image of the brand.

The Super Bowl happens only once a year. The rest of the time, a really successful TV show attracts a maximum audience of only 20 million or, in extremely rare cases, 30 million. Even 30 million is just 10 percent of the population. The venerable Academy Awards, the Super Bowl of fashion, attracts fewer viewers than *American Idol.* That means that the highest-rated programs are still leaving 90 percent of the American people with no knowledge whatsoever of the products or services advertised therein.

Even so, advertising is by no means dead. It still consumes a great deal of money and attention, and far more journalists cover the advertising business than the public relations industry. In fact, most of the largest PR firms are owned by advertising agencies. However, it's crucial to know what each part of an overall marketing campaign can deliver. Advertising can deliver image, frequency, and a pinpointed message. Yet without the PR component, advertising alone lacks credibility, third-party endorsement, and the ability to generate that elusive "buzz" when one person tells another about something spontaneously.

PR is also consistently less expensive than advertising and, on a limited marketing budget, can often be the most cost-effective way to get a message out. You're going to find out how.

That leads us to the subject of public relations. It's not just what you have to offer that matters—it's how you get the word out about who you are, what you are, and what you or your product can do. It's great to be wonderful and to have a terrific product, but what good is it if nobody knows about what it is that you have to offer?

The word "spin" seems to have picked up a negative connotation in our society. People think that it makes us buy things we don't need, watch movies and television shows for the wrong reasons, and love or hate our political candidates. The truth is we all use spin. When we craft a resumé we write about our accomplishments—not our "off days," when we recount our families' weddings we forget the sloppy speech by the drunken best man and focus on the beautiful bride; and we all only want the best photos of us out there; that's spin. It's just another way of saying you're "putting your best foot forward." In fact, much of the image and message research done by companies and political candidates is simply to find out what people care about and what messages will resonate. This forces them to address issues of interest to us.

Spin/PR, or whatever you want to call it, is not just for national brands and national candidates. It's for just about anyone who wants to accomplish almost anything. It's as much a part of everyday life as combing your hair and brushing your teeth, and it's time to start thinking about it because it can change your life.

I don't want to give you the idea that public relations is something new in the world. Actually, the idea of having a "spokesperson" or a "media relations manager" goes at least as far back as the Bible. In the book of Exodus, God commands Moses to appear before the pharaoh and demand, "Let my people go." Moses sought to wriggle out of the assignment and told God that he wasn't particularly articulate. Today, God would have sent him to get some media training. Instead, God told him to bring in his brother Aaron. Essentially he said, "I'll tell you what to say, you tell him, and we'll all be fine." So a lot of us in public relations believe that Aaron is actually the first practitioner of our craft, thus making public relations the third oldest profession, slightly behind spycraft and prostitution. (And we get accused of both of those as well.)

PR always stood for public relations. I believe that in today's world, it actually stands for something different—Perception and Reality. It's the job of a public relations person to form a logical relationship between perception and reality—of an individual, of a product or service, of a geographical entity, of anything. When you think about it, there are really just three possibilities: the public's perception of you may be better than the reality, the reality of your situation may be better than the way the public perceives you, or, ideally, they are in balance. In most cases, for the vast majority of my clients and for most people, their reality is better than the public's perception of them. Perhaps that's because we live in an era where people don't trust anything—they don't trust the media, they don't trust politicians, they don't trust advertisers, and they don't trust a lot of what they read on the Internet. We live in cynical times.

If this is your situation—if you are a better person, or offering a better product, or doing a better job than your public believes or understands about you—how do you create a shift in the public's perception of you so that they accept you and what you offer? How do you get perception and reality in sync? How do you reduce cognitive dissonance—that uncomfortable feeling of juggling two conflicting thoughts at the same time?

This may sound like an abstract concept until you think about how it plays out in the lives of real people. In the workplace, you know you're doing a great job but somebody else gets the promotion or the new job. In an election campaign, you know you've got more to offer than your opponent but he's able to paint you into a corner from which you can't escape—or worse, he defines you before you are able to define yourself. In the marketplace, your product is vastly better than that of your competitor but people are flocking to him. These are make-or-break issues that affect everything from your career to your livelihood to your reputation.

The purpose of this book is to share with you what I've learned working with America's top celebrities, companies, and events—from Frank Sinatra to Stevie Wonder, from Ford to Coca-Cola, to the *Vanity Fair* Oscar party—to show you how to change or create the way people in your world perceive you and what you offer. If you don't define yourself, somebody else is going to define you . . . and not necessarily in a way you like. There's nothing optional, therefore, about taking control of your own public image, and that's what this book is all about.

Another important thing that we will talk about is what to do if the public perception of you or what you offer is actually *better* than your reality. My term for that is "hype." It sounds like a nice place to be, but if the perception of you is better than the reality, you may have further to fall once the reality gets out there. A good PR person monitors the relationship between perception and reality and keeps things in check. In many ways, the term "spin doctor," which is often applied pejoratively to publicists, is quite accurate. The same way a doctor takes the pulse, monitors the heart, the lungs, the blood pressure, and the temperature of a patient, a good PR person takes the pulse of the company or the celebrity status of his or her client to find a baseline: What's their ranking on fan sites? How many Google.com hits do they have? Who likes us and who doesn't? He'll do additional research to find out what the reality is, what the perception is, and what the perception needs to be. We're also in the business of making sure that negative information about our clients doesn't find its way into the media, or if it does, that it is mitigated promptly and powerfully.

Does public relations work every time? Unfortunately, no. Some people have a public perception that cannot be changed, or at least cannot be changed quickly. Take tennis powerhouse John McEnroe. Years ago, when he was still playing professionally, my client Anheuser-Busch was sponsoring tennis exhibitions across the country featuring McEnroe and another player to promote its Michelob Light brand. I traveled with him to a variety of cities to promote the tour. This was at the height of McEnroe's bad-boy era. The exhibitions were more about theater than the actual tennis—the players would emerge onto the court through dry ice smoke with the then–cutting edge song "Boy from New York City" blasting on the sound system.

We held a press conference in each city the day before the event to promote it, and the one in Minneapolis took place in the conference room of a sponsor's department store. The next day, the two local papers—the *Minneapolis Tribune* and the *St. Paul Pioneer Press*—gave us write-ups I'll never forget. One paper said, and I rephrase here, that John McEnroe, "accompanied by a group of slick-looking yes-men, arrived in town yesterday." The other paper described McEnroe's entourage with something like these words: "Better-looking crews have come off fishing trawlers after hurricanes." Let's see—were we slick, or were we just weather-beaten? It didn't matter, because they didn't like John, so they didn't like the people with him; one event was not going to reshape their perception of him.

Sometimes you have no control at all over your image. Two individuals for whom this is true are former vice president Dick Cheney and columnist and conservative gadfly Ann Coulter. In

Cheney's case, he doesn't seem all that perturbed by the fact that people's perception of him is so negative. Or at least if it does bother him, he's not letting on. And who would know anyway, since he spent so much of his vice presidency hidden in a cave. In Ann Coulter's case, she is able to transform every blunder or misstep into an opportunity to raise her public profile. Cheney has transcended caring, while Coulter is intentionally provocative. Coulter believes the bromide that it doesn't matter what they say about you in the newspaper as long as your name is spelled right. Cheney assumes he's above public opinion.

If you're reading this book, it's because you want more than your name spelled right in the paper. It's because you want to either create a perception about you from whole cloth or alter the one that already exists. This is really the difference between revolution (creating a brand new perception) and evolution (changing a perception that's already been out there for some time). Either case takes serious work.

I have learned over the years that there is an inversely proportional relationship between image and risk—that is, the more established the positive image, the less willingness there is to take a risk. Those established companies that do take smart, calculated risks may do okay—except if they fail. Then they're called stupid.

One of the greatest challenges—perhaps the greatest challenge—that a public relations person faces is that he doesn't get to present the client's message directly to the public. Instead, the media serves as a filter, lifting up or burying those whom it favors or dislikes. The media simply doesn't play fair, and objectivity, alas, is a myth. So you can't count on the media to be your friend, to protect you, or to do your bidding, no matter how powerful you may be in your marketplace. Think back to Democratic presidential candidate Michael Dukakis riding in the tank. It's not the photo that cost him the 1988 presidential election. It was the media's incessant playing of the image of Dukakis in the tank that destroyed his presidential ambitions. Granted, he didn't run the most stirring of campaigns, but the media certainly did him no favors by constantly reminding us how silly he looked at the very moment that he was trying to project strength. In politics, this is known as the "macho cred" moment. Why did George W. Bush's flight suit work (at least until the war became unglued) and Michael Dukakis's tank ride fail? It goes back to authenticity: Bush was a pilot, whereas Dukakis rode the subway.

Most people think that, in the 2004 presidential election, Howard Dean imploded and destroyed his own candidacy when he let out that infamous whoop or scream or however you want to categorize it at a campaign rally. The truth is very different. When Dean screamed, he was in a room full of other people who were also whooping and hollering. It wasn't as though he was a perfectly normal guy who had suddenly revealed just how bizarre he was, which is exactly how the media portrayed it. In reality, there were cameras and microphones all over that room, and if you had seen the video from any other angle and listened to the audio as captured by *all* of the mics in the room—not just the one isolated on Dean—you would have heard clearly that *everybody* was screaming. In fact it would be hard to hear Dean at all. By pulling out just the video and audio of Dean screaming into an isolated mic, and neglecting to accurately depict what was really going on, the media created an indelible image of a man far too manic to be trusted with the presidency. Love Dean or hate him, the media's trashing of him in this manner was actually as fraudulent as altering a photo. Through this abusive use of journalistic power, the perception of an unstable Howard Dean instantly became reality. Ironically, he is one of the most stable human beings I've ever met.

Mention Bill Buckner to a sports fan, especially a Boston Red Sox fan, and you'll get anything from rolling eyes to out right contempt. Bill Buckner had enjoyed an outstanding career as a stellar infielder for the Los Angeles Dodgers, but he had never won a World Series ring. In 1986, he found himself at the end of his career playing for the Boston Red Sox, which was making its first real run at a World Series title in more than half a century. With Boston in the lead in the sixth game of the series, Red Sox manager John McNamara elected to leave Buckner at first base in the last innings so that Buckner would have the joy of being on the field as his team won the Series. Unfortunately, the New York Mets' Mookie Wilson hit a ground ball to Buckner, whose knees were in such poor shape that he was unable to bend down and pick up the ball. The ball scooted through his legs and into right field; Wilson was safe on Buckner's error, and the Red Sox promptly lost game six . . . and then the final game seven to the swaggering Mets.

I mention this because very few fans remember Bill Buckner for his outstanding infield play throughout his career. Instead, public perception of Buckner was forever tarnished by that one infield error. Things got so bad for Buckner that he couldn't even remain in Boston, and he ended up moving to the Pacific Northwest, where he now lives. They may treat him right in Idaho, but back in Boston, Bill Buckner's name still lives in infamy. And there's no spin doctor on earth who could revive his image in that city.

But make no mistake—PR works. Especially in the Internet era, when we've gone from a twenty-four-hour news cycle to a twenty-four-second news cycle, you can become famous in a heartbeat. Take Kristine Lefebvre, an attorney in Los Angeles who was a contestant on Donald Trump's television show, *The Apprentice*. Part of Lefebvre's legal work involved negotiating deals with *Playboy* magazine for various celebrities. At one point, she was discussing a particular deal with her counterpart at *Playboy* and the *Playboy* person said, "You're a beautiful woman. You should do *Playboy* yourself." Kristine was married to a European guy, so she received no objection from her husband; a deal was struck, she shed her clothes, and the photo shoot went forward. The shoot turned out so well that *Playboy* even put her on the cover.

Kristine's deal with the magazine was that she would be paid per issue over a certain volume of sales, so she wanted to do some advance PR. On the Friday before the last episode of *The Apprentice*, we leaked to TMZ.com the story of Kristine's upcoming appearance in *Playboy*. As a result, ratings for *The Apprentice* went through the roof, far higher than at any time during the series. If you hadn't been watching all along, there was now only one reason that you were tuning in: because you wanted to see Kristine Lefebvre, the woman who was going to appear on the cover—and inside—*Playboy* magazine. By the following Monday, Kristine Lefebvre was the number one search on AOL. The story also got picked up by the Associated Press, one of the most powerful news organizations in the world, and by practically everyone else in the news media. They all went ballistic . . . viral . . . and gave Kristine every chance for success.

You may not be posing for *Playboy*, but your life is far more likely to be exposed, often in ways you might not like, than ever before. There used to be a wall of privacy both for public figures and for individuals. Not anymore. That wall has come tumbling down with the advent of camera phones, the speed of the Internet, and the ability of people to suss out all sorts of information about practically anyone. The market for celebrity information, scandal, photographs, and video clips has gone through the roof. Everyone from parking valets to lab assistants at hospitals is lured by the temptation to turn information into cold, hard cash.

Television host Kathie Lee Gifford explained it this way: "Privacy is like your health. It's one of those things in life you take completely for granted until it's gone, then you realize how precious it is."

Once Ed McMahon, famous for years as Johnny Carson's sidekick on *The Tonight Show*, had gone to a hospital in Los Angeles for medical tests. He saw the results in the tabloids before he got them from his own doctor.

You don't have to be an Ed McMahon—in the public eye—to be concerned about who's watching you. One of my former clients, Dr. Robert Rey, a plastic surgeon known as "Dr. 90210" on *E! Entertainment*, was criticized by a leading medical journal on the grounds that cameras in operating rooms and doctors' offices were a bad thing, potentially violating the privacy of the patient and posing a threat to the confidentiality of the doctor-patient relationship. The publication was trying to put Dr. Rey on the defensive, so we wrote an op-ed for the journal as a response. I often do op-eds (bylined pieces that appear on the page opposite the editorial page of newspapers) in situations like this, combining my client's ideas and my take on the topic. My job is to write it in their voice, as best I can. This particular opinion piece said that if you're a physician, whether you're in your own office or the operating room, you ought to be acting at all times as if there were a camera over your shoulder. Why shouldn't people know what you are doing? It's actually the best thing for medicine, because it will cut down on malpractice. In the age of spin, like it or not, we all can be on *Candid Camera.*

Why am I writing this book? Because my career in many ways has paralleled the explosion of the field of public relations and I want to share what I've learned with the widest possible audience. I see a lack of basic communication skills. I see people wanting to be famous for just being famous. I see loyalty ebbing, being replaced by cynicism. Again and again, I see people going on TV just because they can, not because they should.

By the very nature of what we do, PR people are educators. We educate media about clients, and we educate our clients about the media. I educate and mentor my younger staff about how to do PR more successfully. I've had the honor of teaching PR at the University of Southern California and explaining it in terms that college students can understand. Now I want to share my thirty years' experience with you.

A while back I was doing PR for a Budweiser Parade of Stars Concert to benefit the United Negro College Fund. The day before the concert I placed a huge story on it in the local paper, the *Flint Journal.* My grandmother read the paper and called me.

"What a coincidence," she remarked. "You're here for a concert and there's a huge article on it in the paper."

"I did that," I replied.

"You did what?" she asked.

"I got that article in the paper."

"So," she asked, confused, "where's your name?"

So where's *your* name? How are you perceived in your world? Do decision makers—consumers, voters, bosses, customers—understand who you are and what you offer? You can't be hiding your light under a bushel basket in today's world and hope to succeed. In Hollywood there is an axiom: Doing the work is half the job. The other half is making sure that your work is seen and promoted in this cluttered marketplace. What's your reality and what do people think about you? Are they aligned? If the perception of you isn't where you want it to be, what do you have to do to transform it so that you maximize your influence, sales, success, income, or any combination thereof?

Sometimes people ask me how I got into this field. In college, I worked for a small Ann Arbor ad agency. Once I graduated and began interviewing for advertising jobs in New York and Chicago, they kept asking me, "Are you a suit or are you a creative?"—meaning, do you intend to make your career in advertising on the business side, working with clients, or on the creative side, designing the ads?

I had been doing both at the small agency during my college years. I didn't know I had to choose.

"I think I can do both," I replied.

"No, you can't," they told me. "You've got to choose sides."

"I like working with clients," I said, "and I also think I'm creative. I think I can write ads pretty well."

"Sorry," they told me. "You've got to choose."

So I chose to leave. I got a writing job at a small society magazine, *Chicago Elite*, put out by the owner of a successful gun dealer magazine because his wife wanted to go to a better class of parties. I submitted one story, and they didn't change a word. I felt really smart. I submitted a second story, and they didn't change a word on that one either. I felt even smarter. Then they didn't change a word on the third story. And I thought to myself, "I'm not that smart." If they weren't interested in "growing" me as a writer, then maybe this wasn't the right place for me. The magazine folded after a year and I got a job with a small PR agency in Chicago. I thought to myself that it couldn't be that hard—it seemed that half of the people who had pitched me stories at the magazine hadn't even bothered to read the publication. In the public relations world, former journalists are welcome. They figure that we know how to pitch stories because we've been pitched to for so long.

The company soon won Anheuser-Busch as a client. I was twenty-four years old at the time, and suddenly I was traveling to ten different states on behalf of the biggest beer company in the world. Every weekend there was another event to support with publicity. Anheuser-Busch was a great client—they loved publicity, they understood how to maximize sponsorships, and they were willing to spend money. I learned a lot from them and I am very grateful to them for essentially giving me an MBA in PR. I then took a job at Burson-Marsteller, which was the largest PR firm in the world at the time, because I wanted to play in a bigger arena. I remained friends with the people there, who mentored me as I started my own company. I had truly found my home in public relations. I knew after my first week that I loved my profession.

Edward Bernays, often known as "the father of public relations," said a PR person has three jobs: first, and most obvious, present the client to the public; second, interpret the public for the client (what's the landscape the client is entering); and finally, and perhaps most important, do good.

There are a lot of different names for what we do. You can call us publicists, flacks, media relations managers, image consultants, spin doctors, spokespeople, press secretaries, crisis managers, or some combination thereof. Whatever you want to call us, the techniques we use will work just as well in your world as they do in mine. There's no question about it—we live in the age of spin. So spin along with me; as you develop, change, or protect your own image, you'll be in for the ride of your life.

CHAPTER 2

GOING TO THE NEXT LEVEL

Who needs PR?

Who needs to create or reshape a personal image or the image of his or her company or brand? In short, who's this book for?

In three decades of listening to clients tell me why they've come into my office, one phrase comes through again and again—*they want to go to the next level.*

What's the next level in *your* life? Higher income? More recognition? A promotion? Winning an election? Converting others to your way of thinking about politics, the environment, or some other idea or cause? However you define success in your sphere, if you're trying to reach that elusive next level, you must manage the perceptions others have of you, your product, or your service. Don't believe that stuff about the world beating a path to the door of the person with a better mousetrap. The world, in fact, will beat a path to the person who sets out enough cheese . . . for the media.

Who's reaching for the next level? A doctor specializing in a hot area of medicine. A lawyer who has won a big settlement and wants to use that case as a stepping stone in his career. A business getting ready to expand. A celebrity about to appear in an attention-getting role in a new film. A community activist running for public office. An educator or PTA president who wants to start changing things on a macro, not micro, level. An environmentalist who wants to start a nonprofit and change the world.

One of the biggest problems facing businesses today is called "commoditization"—a phenomenon linked to the belief that "all companies are created equal" and "all products and services are created equal." In a world where every product or service is viewed as a commodity, the only way companies can differentiate themselves is in terms of price. In other words, the world doesn't care how good you, your service, or your product might be; it just cares how cheap it is. The only way to overcome commoditization is to find a way to stand out. PR helps you do just that.

It's not just seemingly faceless businesses that fear being commoditized in the marketplace. Even celebrities fear it. I had a conversation recently with the beautiful host of a nightly entertainment show. She told me, "I think we're all interchangeable blondes after a while, and I don't want to be that anymore." The last thing you want to be is interchangeable. PR illustrates the differences between you and those against whom you are competing.

People often come to me for the wrong reason—they want to be famous. I tell them fame is not the goal, recognition is. Fame will come as a by-product of recognition.

People come to me when they see articles or TV stories about their competitors. They tell me indignantly, "I do more business than they do." Or, "I'm more articulate." Or, "I'm more deserving." All these questions boil down to two simple words—*where's mine?* Public relations can be the golden key to getting what's yours.

PR is also for those who have made a change in their life and need the world to know it. It might be an actor reinventing his image after a public failure by shaking up his team, hiring a new agent, manager, or publicist, and taking on a challenging role. In the life of a private person, it might be a personal change—a breakup, a divorce, a new marriage or relationship. Or it might be about a business, individual, or brand coming back after a challenging period. It might be a company opening a new office in another city; landing a big account; or acquiring a competitor.

Another person whose image would need rehabilitation would be someone coming out of jail. Martha Stewart handled her comeback from insider-trading changes beautifully. Jail softened her image. But how did she end up in jail in the first place? Stewart built a billion-dollar brand, but she didn't build along with it a foundation of charity and caring, or if she did, she didn't promote it enough. When she got in trouble, who was there to stand up for her? Who was there to give her the benefit of the doubt? If you're going to be highly successful, and if your success is going to be in the public eye, you've got to create an image for yourself that says, "I care about people other than myself and I care about more than just simply being rich."

Compare Martha Stewart's legal troubles with those of Oprah Winfrey. When Oprah got in trouble with the beef producers, everybody rushed to her side. That's because she had already developed an image as a person who genuinely cared. By contrast, we never saw the "Martha Stewart House for Wayward Girls." Of course, all of a sudden, her house became the "Home for *a* Wayward Girl."

Martha Stewart's situation shows that you *can* go home again (the tenth of my Ten Commandments of PR which you will find at the end of the book). She knitted a poncho in jail. She humanized herself. She was humiliated, and we felt her pain, and we like her better now. The public consensus now on Martha Stewart is that she was a victim of the government—a notch on the belt of an overzealous prosecutor, not a true miscreant.

These are all situations in which a well-thought-out publicity campaign can make a difference. One of my basic premises about public relations, however, is that just because you *can* get press doesn't mean you *should* get press. Just about everybody has the ability to get press in today's media-saturated culture. But a media campaign has to be part of a bigger picture.

Talk show host Rita Crosby came out with a book about Larry Birkhead, the father of the late Anna Nicole Smith's baby. As much as it hurts to have your reputation maligned in a book, Larry chose to go on a number of talk shows to defend himself and refute her charges. I think he would have been better served by judicious silence than fueling the controversy of the book and increasing attention and sales.

I was disappointed by Larry's judgment when he took his child for a walk down L.A.'s Robertson Boulevard., the street with the highest number of paparazzi, having dressed her in a T-shirt that read, "Who's your daddy?" His child had become a prop. And when he cut a deal with a magazine to sell pictures of the kid's birthday party, he was using his child as his ATM. It's just not right; children are not props or cash cows.

Larry focused a lot of energy on talking to the media. He liked the limelight and enjoyed having a relationship with journalists known to all of America by their first names. But ultimately, is that the best thing for him, his image, or his relationship with his daughter? I don't think so. Does a person want to be known as a tabloid husband, part of a circus act, or someone who is a good father with a good career?

If you are involved in a nationally newsworthy situation, don't be surprised when the "first-name journalists" come calling. But don't consider them your new "friends" in the media. "Friends" in the media are not your friends. Don't let your strategy be built around supposed "friendships" like these. These journalists and their staffs are not there ultimately to be your friend, even though they can be amazingly charming. They are people with a job to do, and they'll use you and then move on. Don't fall into the trap of thinking that now that you're "famous" you get to hobnob with the Geraldos of the world. That's not the way it works.

Another example of a person who did not benefit from publicity, even though her situation offered her plenty of opportunities for publicity, was the first runner-up in the 2007 Miss USA pageant. Pageant director Donald Trump, you may recall, went live on national television to announce, in dramatic terms, his forgiveness of the winner of the pageant, who had gotten into trouble in some New York clubs. Trump told a breathless television audience that Miss USA was ultimately a good girl who had made some mistakes. So now everyone wanted to know what the first runner-up had to say, since she would have taken the title had Trump bounced the winner of the competition.

Her best move would have been to not seek any media coverage and instead just put out a statement—something to the effect of, "I'm happy for her. Anyone would want a second chance." And then she should let the whole thing go. Instead, the young lady went on numerous television shows and looked very self-serving and perhaps even bitter. I don't think the appearances helped her, and she certainly has not parlayed her experiences into a significant television or movie career of any sort yet. She didn't build anything. Again, just because you *can* get publicity doesn't mean you *should*.

You might be saying, "Howard, I know I want publicity, and I know I need it. Tell me how to write a really killer press release already."

I don't mean to disappoint you, but this isn't a book about how to write press releases. You can find plenty of those on the shelves already. Instead, this is a book to help you think about popular culture and your place in it, and to think about your community, whether it's local, national, or international, and your place in it. The main questions I want you to think about for now are these:

> Who do you want to be in the world?
>
> How do you want people to think of you?
>
> How do you want to be known?
>
> If you could define your legacy—and you can—
> what would your legacy be?

I grew up in Flint, Michigan, the town made famous by Michael Moore and his documentary *Roger and Me*, about General Motors. Most of the parents of the kids I knew when I was growing up worked in factories. These were good kids, but they were not especially aspirational. They expected to put the same kinds of bolts into Buicks on the assembly line as had their fathers and grandfathers before them. Back then, GM workers were well compensated, well taken care of, and enjoyed good benefits. But there were others in town who wanted more.

Somebody in Flint must have grown up wanting to be the president of General Motors. Or the union organizer. Or the author of a book. Perhaps you remember an excellent book called *Rivethead*, written by Ben Hamper, which told the story of what it was like to work on the line at GM. To me, this illustrates the fact that out of every hundred people, only a few have aspirations greater than those dictated for them by their surroundings. Are you one of those people?

Some people are addicted to seeing themselves in the media. Britney Spears might be one of those people. It's been said that the definition of an extrovert is someone for whom nothing happens until someone else knows about it. Some people, quite frankly, are a little too extroverted for their own good. If you're going to melt down, don't do it in front of the media. I go on CNN a lot, and for a while I was asked frequently about Britney Spears. "If you were Britney's PR guy," they would ask, "how would you fix her problems?"

"She doesn't have PR problems," I would respond. "She has life problems."

We have to understand the difference between PR and life: the truth seeks its own level. That's another of my Ten Commandments of PR. If your public image is out of order, we can fix it, but if you're out there doing terrible things, all the PR in the world isn't going to make a difference.

So let's say you've got a legitimate reason (or even an illegitimate reason; who am I to judge?) for creating a PR campaign. How do you know that you, or what you offer, will be a good candidate for a publicity campaign? I'd like to offer four criteria. If you meet any of these, you're probably in.

1. *Do you have enough money?* If you have enough money, you can generate attention. It's that simple. The greater your aspirations—the broader the canvas on which you want to operate—the more it's going to cost. But if you want to pay the piper and spend your money wisely, the media will happily dance to your tune.

2. *Does your offering make sense?* Let's say you import a particular Italian beer. Germany, the Netherlands, and the United Kingdom are the countries in Europe best known for beer, with Belgium and France not far behind them. (Okay, quite far behind them, but that's another discussion.) But Italy? How many Italian beers can you name? So you have a great idea to promote your Italian beer: you'll make bocci, the Italian bowling game, the next great American sport. Now, the market for beer is men, so you want to get in the sports pages. The only problem is that most American newspapers don't have a bocci reporter. The newspapers in Florence? They might. Here, not so much. Who on earth is going to write your bocci stories?

It's never gonna happen. Instead of bocci, pick an Italian soccer star as a spokesperson for your beer. Or better yet, since you are seeking to appeal to American men, pick a beautiful Italian actress. You've got a much better chance of someone writing about soccer or Italian actresses than about bocci. Of course, I've been wrong before and maybe you will turn bocci into an international phenomenon. But in the meantime, there's got to be a sensible connection between what you're offering and what the media can comfortably translate into a public image.

Keep in mind that media stories have to be "slotted"—they've got to fit into already established categories. A plane can't just take off from Detroit and land at LAX. It's got to have a slot at the airport—a time when it can land and find an open gate. Your story has to somehow "slot" or make sense to whatever media you are seeking to cover it.

3. *Are you passionate about what you're doing?* Is your issue or cause something to stir and inspire the world? Can it lift and motivate people? The more passionate you are about your offering, and the more passion you can inspire in others, the more likely you are to succeed. I recently saw a food called Plumpy'nut featured on *60 Minutes*. It's a combination of peanuts, milk, and vitamins, and it is literally ending malnutrition among children in impoverished regions of the world. Kids love the taste and the product is saving lives. Another innovation—the XO-1, an inexpensive laptop for children designed by the social welfare organization One Laptop Per Child (OLPC)—was developed to provide access to knowledge to kids in developing countries. Can you get passionate about products like these? I think you can. Is your product or idea powerful enough to inspire passion in the world you seek to influence? Environmental activists are doing it every day.

Passion must be a two-way street. It's not enough that what you offer excites you. It's got to excite *others* as well. Back when I was at Burson-Marsteller, we were having a brainstorming meeting to discuss the market introduction of Procter & Gamble's new product, Liquid Tide. For P&G, of course, Tide is a flagship brand, so when Tide goes liquid, it's a big deal—just like Coca-Cola creating Diet Coke. In that meeting I asked, "Does the client understand that while it's culture-changing in their world, it might not matter very much in the real world?" People stared at me for a while, because I was speaking heresy. But when you think about it, it makes sense: if it didn't matter to you, you wouldn't be thinking about publicizing it, but will it matter to anyone else?

4. *Finally, could this be a foot in the door to something greater?* Not every single project or activity represents your life's dreams and greatest ambitions. Sometimes we do things because we know—or at least we hope—that they will lead to greater things down the road. When we launched Fresca for Coca-Cola, that wasn't a particularly big project. A lot of work, and not a lot of profit. But it was our chance to show the client what we could do. If the idea you want to publicize represents a stepping-stone toward greater things, then by all means go for it.

Who needs PR? Anyone who has a good reason for taking his or her image, career, product, or service to the next level. Who doesn't need PR? Anyone who could benefit more from judicious silence than media saturation. How can you tell if PR is right for you? If you've got the money, if you've got a sensible idea, if you're passionate, or if this project represents a step on the path to greater things, then go for it. It's time for your fifteen minutes.

There are three important things to learn about PR right off the bat. First, PR is a process, not a blueprint. Second, it's a marathon, not a sprint. And most important, everybody's DNA plays differently in the public arena. Why does Ann Coulter turn into a pariah when she calls John Edwards a "faggot" . . . but Jerry Lewis can drop the F-bomb on his telethon with nary a bleep?

Just remember that recognition is not an end point—it's currency that you can spend any way you see fit. Fame is what fame can do for you. George Clooney calls fame a credit card to change the world. For others, it can be a way to build respect, step up a career, make money, or get laid. Some use fame to further their activism. Others use it to stay in the public eye even when they shouldn't. Fame can also be a pain: when you're picking your nose while driving or if you're rude to a waiter, everyone on the planet is going to know about it. You'll be judged harshly—count on it. A famous woman stepping out of her home to jog wearing no makeup and dressed in sweatpants can open the tabloids a few days later and . . . hello. Is that really *me*?

Fame is a bitch goddess. It can help you or it can destroy you. But if you can approach it sensibly, it can open doors for you in unimaginable ways. So let's start opening some doors for you.

CHAPTER 3

TAKING THE PULSE

Anyone with enough money, cunning, or guile, let alone a good reason, can get on the cover of *Time, People*, or pretty much any other magazine. The question is this: are you willing to do what it takes to get there?

Maybe you don't need the cover of *Time* or *Newsweek* to attain your dream. But whether you're trying to reach *People* magazine or just the people down the block, the first step in putting together a public relations strategy is to *take the pulse of your current public image.*

What makes you you? Who are you authentically? Who are your friends? Who are your enemies? In today's world, there are a lot of people whose agenda is hate and destruction. They launch computer viruses, start wildfires, or just have negative things to say about people — which they publish on the Internet. We call them "haters."

More than ever, you really need to know who's with you and who's against you. Whenever I'm working with a new client, I turn immediately to the Internet, because there are shocking amounts of free information online about almost everyone. Our desire here is to get a baseline so we can understand exactly what your image is right now. This allows you to be realistic about where your image can go. Most people think public relations is about puffery and exaggeration, but in fact, authenticity is the most important fundamental in public relations—and it is also the starting point.

You may have heard of opposition research—where a political campaign digs out all the scurrilous information it can find about the opposing candidate. Did you know that campaigns also perform this kind of opposition research on their own candidates? Consulting firms will search out everything that's been written about a candidate. That way they already know the negatives and can prepare responses. The last thing a campaign candidate or his staff wants is to be blindsided by some piece of information that the candidate has failed to reveal. As long as it's all on the table, the spokesperson can immediately choose an appropriate response instead of scrambling to find out the truth. The spokesperson can say, "It's not true," or, "That happened forty-eight years ago," or, "We've discussed that already." If you don't know what people are saying about you already, how can you expect to affect what they'll believe about you later on?

Realism is essential. Some celebrities live in never-never land. You can't ascribe rational thought to their behavior when they are motivated emotionally. But celebrities don't have a hammerlock on distorted thinking. Lots of regular people suffer from it too. Public relations is going to help you only if you can be realistic about who you are, what you've done, and how you are currently perceived. Maybe you can spin every negative about you, but there comes a point where you have to say, "I've got fifty negative articles about me on the Internet. Is there anything I can do to fix this?"

So the first part of taking the pulse is finding out what's out there so that you can be realistic about who you are and what you've done. But what if there's nothing about you on the Internet? Then take the pulse of your public image among your friends. Don't ask them, "What do you think of me?" Instead, ask them to identify your assets, your accomplishments, your fans, and your enemies. You're trying to create a balance sheet of your image, identifying assets and liabilities. Are we building your new image on a strong foundation, or is the foundation a little shaky?

Here's an example. A physician who had accomplished great things in medical research and political fund-raising was at the end stage of a terminal illness. A friend of mine, David Kessler, a renowned expert on end-of-life issues, was working with him in this period of final transition. There was some talk of doing a story about him, to honor him as he reached the end of his life. Unfortunately, research revealed some unflattering legal problems that he had encountered earlier in his life. The reporters told us, "He did some good things, but I found some negatives too. If I do the story, it'll all have to be in there."

The media is not in the business of giving people a free pass. Reporters are all about presenting stories in a balanced fashion, or at least appearing to present stories that are balanced. That means that negatives about you are as likely to appear as positives. If the negatives outweigh the message you're trying to get across, then you may need to control the message—not through media but through the use of ads, direct mail, or other approaches. If there are too many negatives that the media would feel obliged (or perhaps delighted) to report, then public relations may not be for you.

A major benefit of public relations is that media coverage can provide a third-party endorsement. If you say you're a good guy, and if your mother says you're a good guy, that's one thing. But if the *New York Times* says so, all of America is going to believe it. (Okay, most of America.) That's because all credible media outlets are based on the concept of "balance." They have to put the bad in with the good. They don't have to put in a lot of bad to make a story work, but they have to put in some. It's rare to find a major outlet doing a major story and presenting it as entirely positive or entirely negative. You've got to have balance. If a leading newspaper or magazine tells a story, people assume that it's credible . . . because they consider both sides of the issue. Are they always fair? Are they always accurate? Wanna buy a bridge? But the major outlets confer credibility when they do stories about people, products, services, or businesses.

So far, we've been talking about a brand—whether of an individual or a product or service—that already exists in the marketplace. That's evolutionary PR. By contrast, revolutionary PR is when you are launching something that's brand new or feels brand new. My friend Burton Morris is a Pop artist. Burton's work could be described as Andy Warhol and Roy Lichtenstein meet Keith Haring. I would call his stunning work evolutionary rather than revolutionary because he is building on the creations of artists who have gone before him while still creating his own unique style. So what's revolutionary?

Not long before I began this book, a new frozen yogurt called Pinkberry exploded onto the scene. It's your basic frozen yogurt—not much new there—but Pinkberry was marketed as a revolutionary experience in the world of dessert. Is Pinkberry evolutionary or revolutionary? You can ask the people standing in long lines stretching down the block for the product; people in the business might tell you it's evolutionary, but people who actually eat the stuff think it's brand new.

What if you are seeking to present to the world a product, service, or personal image that is, in fact, brand new? You've got a clean slate. That's a positive—there's nothing negative out there about your offering. The bad news is also that there's nothing out there—nothing in the minds of the public about the thing you wish to publicize. If you or what you're offering is not very well known, it'll be your responsibility to educate the media as to what you are or what you stand for.

Companies with established brands start with their existing reputation as leverage for talking about their new image and their new vision of who they are in the marketplace. Companies, individuals, politicians, actors and actresses, or anyone else in the public eye cannot deny their past. When Spiegel sought to upgrade its catalogue, it couldn't sweep decades of history under a polyester rug. Spiegel had to start off by saying, "This is who we have always been. Now how do we want to position ourselves in the minds of consumers?"

Whatever you're offering, when you're taking the pulse of an image in the marketplace, it's all about recognizing what, if anything, is already out there. The Internet is the starting point, but there's plenty of research still to be done. "Primary research" means going out and doing your own homework on how people feel about your "brand." Look at the polls that TV news organizations conduct online each day. That is primary quantitative research. Let's say you were thinking about Madonna as a spokesperson for a product you offer. You can convene a focus group to find out how she would fare. When I do focus groups, we gather ten or fifteen people at random to elicit feelings about Madonna and perhaps about the product as well. I want to know how people feel. The feeling might be positive, as in "Whatever she's wearing, I would wear." Or "I think her time is over. I'd rather follow somebody younger or somebody not as controversial." (Focus groups are primary *qualitative* research. When news organizations conduct polls and then the newscaster reads the letters people send in to explain their votes, those letters are also qualitative.)

You can also do a survey to determine what percentage of people like, admire, and trust Madonna. Your results can be qualitative—"I think she's really creative ... hot ... inspirational" ... whatever—or quantitative, which includes anything that's given in a percentage. Let's say your study finds that 68 percent of Americans believe that Madonna is a good mother—well, now you have something to go by.

There's no substitute for doing your own homework to see how an activity of yours in the marketplace would fare. Focus groups may not be perfect—there were probably focus groups that gave their blessings to New Coke and Crystal Pepsi (everybody has an off day once in a while)—but the information they generate is invariably helpful in creating a campaign.

In addition to primary research, there's secondary research, which involves using existing sources. We've already talked about the Web, so now it's time to look through magazines, books, medical journals (if appropriate), and other already-published sources of information to learn more about how your offering is viewed by the marketplace.

Here's a different issue. Let's say you're already in the public eye for one thing. Does that mean you have to stay slotted in that same place forever? Absolutely not. It doesn't matter how you got famous—once you're a celebrity and you have your own fame to deal with, you can often move on and be famous for something else. Something may be part of your history, but not part of your message today. Tom Arnold became famous by being married to Roseanne Barr. It doesn't matter today that this was his first step into the limelight. Once he got there, he stayed there, and served as the host of the long-running talk show *Best Damn Sports Show,* as well as a working actor. Did his marriage to Roseanne come up frequently on the show? Doubtful. Does a generation of viewers who know him only as the host of that show, or as an actor in his own right, even remember that he once was married to Roseanne? Again, doubtful.

For those of us who are not known to the world by our first names, the same rule applies: we can be known for one thing and then seek to develop our careers in a different direction. For example, an individual who starts a successful business in her city may decide to parlay that fame into a campaign to become the city's mayor. You get to reinvent yourself in this great country of ours.

However, it's not always so easy. One of the dominant trends in mass entertainment today is the reality show, and many winners on such shows have tried to jump to fame in other venues. It's very hard for most of them to do so because there are more famous people in the world than there are opportunities for people to be in the public eye. Every year, more people become famous, making it difficult for even well-known people to cut through the clutter and find or keep an audience.

Nevertheless, some people have spun reality television fame

into career gold. Elisabeth Hasselbeck was a *Survivor* contestant before she became a regular on *The View*. Dr. Joyce Brothers parlayed a run as a contestant on the 1950s-era TV game show *The $64,000 Question* into an iconic career as an on-air psychologist. The new millennium's version of Dr. Brothers, Dr. Phil, had the best launching pad for a career this side of Cape Canaveral—Oprah Winfrey. When Oprah was hauled into court by the Texas Cattlemen's Association after airing her show on the dangers of mad cow disease in American slaughterhouses, Dr. Phil was her jury consultant. She was so impressed with him that she developed his TV show, which led to a media empire for Dr. Phil and other members of his family.

More proof, if you need it, that just about anyone can be plucked from obscurity to celebrity is K-Fed. He's an actor/dancer, known on his driver's license as Kevin Federline, who had the questionable fortune of marrying and producing children with Britney Spears. K-Fed is doing everything the right way—he's trying to improve his acting and music careers while at the same time demonstrating to the movie-going public (as well as the divorce court) that he is a good dad. By the time you read this, K-Fed could be a megastar or the answer to a Hollywood trivia question. Frankly, fatherhood is more important than being an international superstar. What's most glamorous is not always the most important.

So anyone can become famous, we would have to conclude. But it's not enough to know how others feel about you as you begin your campaign. Establishing a baseline also means understanding the nuances of the world you are entering. You've got to understand where the audience is, what the trends are, and what misconceptions in society might affect the way you are perceived. When I taught college, I may have learned more than many of my students, because I would typically bring into the classroom a number of experts on a given topic and let them debate, Oprah-style, their points of view before an audience of students. For example, since illegal downloading has been a big topic for years and a hot-button issue for younger people, I

brought in someone from the Recording Industry Association of America (RIAA), which protects the rights of artists and
producers, and someone from Scour.com, a master-like service
that allowed people to download practically anything (it has
since been shut down). Obviously, these two individuals represented points of view that were so irreconcilable that they nearly
came to blows in my classroom. I loved that class.

I learned from the discussion that college kids don't want to
pay for content on the Internet. Artists' rights hold no interest
to young people. Their attitude is that if it's out there on the Internet, it ought to be on their laptop, desktop, or PDA at no additional charge. What about musicians who spend a lot of time
and money creating and recording songs? "They can make
money from concerts" was the typical response. So if you're going to try to sell information or any kind of content on the Internet to an audience of eighteen- to thirty-four-year-olds, you've
got to know that their view of copyright issues is very different
from that of their elders. I was aiming for an Oprah-like experience in my classroom; instead, I nearly ended up with Jerry
Springer.

As long as we're talking about age groups, let's shatter another common myth—that eighteen- to thirty-four-year-olds represent the most alluring audience for advertisers. That's hardly
true. People in their forties, fifties, and up have a heck of a lot
more disposable income than younger people—and they often
dispose of it quite freely. Frankly, the eighteen-to-thirty-four-
year-old demographic may be overrated. The point of this part
of the discussion isn't so much to do with artists' rights or de-
mographics. It's that you need to know a lot about the world you
are entering or reentering, and if you don't, you'll be spending a
lot of time, money, and effort with no upside.

To stay abreast of things, you must consume media. You've
got to know what's out there: what kinds of magazines, TV, and
radio programs are interested in issues like yours, and what interviewers or publications you might want to court and which
ones you might want to avoid. Kay Bailey Hutchison, the Repub-

lican senator from Texas, went on Bill Maher's show not too long ago. Bad idea—ultimately, Bill Maher's is a humor show, and she wasn't funny. If you're boring, you're not achieving your goals. If you go on any show, or if you allow yourself to be interviewed by any outlet inappropriate for your message, it won't serve you well. Years ago, a "family values" senator from the South gave an interview to *Genesis* magazine. Imagine his embarrassment—and the snickers of his detractors—when *Genesis* turned out to be not a biblical journal but a skin magazine. Once the article appeared, there wasn't a fig leaf in America big enough for the senator to hide behind.

The economy could also affect your ability to get your story out. Let's say you wanted to publicize a real estate venture you were creating. While I was writing this book, real estate was in a downturn. So the real estate sections of Sunday newspapers were smaller than those times when real estate is booming. Fewer ads for real estate translate into shorter real estate sections, and that translates into less room for stories about real estate. So it's important to pay attention to trends in the marketplace you seek to penetrate.

Here's another issue to consider: if you haven't been around for a while and you're making a comeback, tell us where you've been. Reintroductions are a critical part of public relations as well. Just recently, I handled the reintroduction to the marketplace of an actress who had taken about fifteen years away from Hollywood. The message that I crafted for her: "I'm a working actress in my forties and I have great kids. I look great, especially for someone my age." We never had her saying that in exactly those words, but we got that message across.

Incidentally, one of the most popular topics in the world is when people change their looks. When Ricki Lake lost all her weight and became a size 2–4, we got cover offers from three magazines—*US, OK!,* and *People*—in just one week. So a crash media campaign could well begin with a crash diet.

If you've taken the suggestions in this chapter, you now have an overall picture of your "reputational health." You've taken the pulse, and that dictates the course of treatment. We're not always good at being realistic about ourselves, which is why it's important to have someone, whether it's a PR professional or simply a trusted friend or adviser, at your side. You've now learned how the world feels about you through the Internet and other secondary sources, through "opposition research" on yourself to see what negatives might exist about you; through focus groups or other traditional marketing approaches; and through additional primary and secondary research. Now that you've taken the pulse, it's time to craft a vision of exactly where you want your image to go, and that's the subject of the next chapter.

CHAPTER 4

CRAFTING YOUR VISION

When creating your vision of the image you wish to present to the world, cook it in a Crock-Pot, not a microwave. Microwaves make things hot and steamy quickly, but when you go to consume them, they aren't tasty—they're rubbery, not evenly cooked. PR, like cooking, is alchemy. Put chicken, some liquids, and some seasoning into a pot, and what you take out is better than what you put in. Similarly, in PR, cooking up a new reputation requires following established recipes . . . but then also adding in your own personal flavoring.

Your vision for your image may have nothing to do with what the world already thinks about you. All of us are born with a public image—we can be "born into a good family," or in a crack house, or anywhere in between. We might be remembered by our relatives as a happy baby, a cranky baby, dictatorial, or complacent. Whatever we were, the question is, now, who do we want to be? And if we want our image to stick—or, to go back to the kitchen for a metaphor, if we want our image soufflé to rise—the most important thing is *authenticity*.

Authenticity simply means that the image or message you

present is consistent with who you really are. Consider these two examples. A woman whose mother has breast cancer is at an event supporting the effort to find a cure. As she is talking to reporters on the press line, she's saying, "My mother has this disease, and I know the courage it takes to fight it." Contrast that scene with a celebrity at that same breast cancer event, saying, "This is a huge women's issue, and I'm proud to be here." She's got no story to tell. It doesn't mean she doesn't belong there. But it would make better sense—and people would be saying "Yeah, I'll buy this"—if she had some authentic connection to the event she is using as a vehicle for self-promotion.

If you're going to buy what the person is selling, you've got to buy the fact that the person is right to sell that product in the first place. Would Nicole Kidman make it as a spokesmodel for Suave shampoo? Probably not, because she's not thought of as a bargain-priced actress and Suave is a bargain brand. What about Chanel? Anyone viewing such an ad would say that makes sense. The Suave campaign wouldn't make sense for either the actress or the shampoo, whereas the Chanel campaign enhances the reputation of both—because it feels authentic for a megastar like Kidman to promote a product like that.

Sometimes people unknowingly give off subtle hints that they don't really belong in a particular situation, that a situation is inauthentic for them. I remember a megamerger years ago between two huge media companies. The CEO of one company wore a standard-issue jacket and tie and looked very corporate. His counterpart from the other media conglomerate wore a brown sport coat with an open shirt. It struck me that this was not going to be a marriage made in heaven; the opposing signals that the men's attire sent indicated, at least to me, that this was probably a relationship that wasn't going to work. And in fact it did not.

Creating an image for the media and the public is a lot like dating. If you're dating and you think you have to be someone you're not, it won't work. The truth will come out. When you craft your vision of who you want to be in the world, be authentic. Be realistic. And if you don't take the time to define yourself at the beginning, someone else will—namely, your competition. If you don't define yourself, it will serve the purposes of your opponent to define you in a negative way. You never want others to define you.

Are you clear about what exactly your new offering is? I recently met with executives of a new movie production company. They confidently explained what defined the movies they would produce, the budget, and other critical issues. I thought to myself, These people get it, and I can support their vision in the marketplace; they know who they are and they know what they want to do. In Mickey Rooney/Judy Garland terms, it's not, "Hey, kids. Let's put on a show." Instead, it's, "We're going to put on a show involving four men, four women, eight songs, four dance numbers, and a female solo that's going to knock the audience's socks off." Your vision doesn't have to be precise down to the last millimeter, but we have to have a pretty good idea of exactly what you want people to know.

You also want to be on guard against overreaching, because people don't like that. The marketplace will generally grant you just one vision at a time. When Hillary Rodham Clinton was running for senator in New York, she was always coy about the issue of the presidency. If she had come right out and said, "Look, people. The whole purpose of running for the Senate from your state is so that I can become president someday," they would have laughed her out of the Big Apple. Let people get to know you and your vision one step at a time.

Similarly, a client of mine, the CEO of a travel company, wanted to broaden her firm into a lifestyle brand. Unfortunately, she moved too quickly and started losing money on the core travel business. As a result, she was fired. Now the company is focusing on its core and doing well again. Once they have their rhythm back, they'll consider other things, and that's the right way to do it.

Your vision has to be realistic and credible not just to you but to the people whom you seek to influence. Want to move from a seat on the city council to governor or U.S. senator? Probably not going to happen. What about from city counselor to mayor or state representative? That will probably work. Know your next step. It's fine to think many moves ahead on the chessboard, but as far as the world is concerned, make only one visible move at a time.

These days, everybody wants to launch a successful social networking Web site and sell it for a gazillion dollars. But who are you going to get to populate your site? You might want to be able to tell investors, "I have two million people." But those two million people are two million individuals who don't care about your ambitions and don't want to be one of your statistics.

A better approach: "This is a social networking site that understands the lives of busy, hardworking professionals and allows them to meet others who match that description in a safe, comfortable setting." That's a lot better than saying "If we get a whole bunch of high-income people to sign on somehow, we can sell it down the road for a big multiple." The marketplace must feel comfortable with your vision.

So how do you reach for something more? You can create a self-fulfilling prophecy about yourself. Early in her career, Cameron Diaz was a model becoming an actress. When we represented her at the time of her first major film role in *The Mask*, our job was to paint her as more than a model. We wanted to depict her as someone with a great future in Hollywood, so we did a story showcasing her entire team—her publicist, her manager, and her agent—to demonstrate that she was in Hollywood for the long haul. Today, Cameron Diaz is one of the most bankable stars in Hollywood, a leap that few models have been able to make. And unlike so many in Hollywood, she has remained shockingly loyal to her original team. She's smart enough to know that her looks and talent will only succeed with a strong team.

The fact that Diaz's team helped her achieve that goal demonstrates that everything is collaborative; there are few people who make huge successes of themselves without the help of others. Once people become successful and famous, they often like to rewrite history and pretend that they did it all by themselves. But let's not kid ourselves; a lot of people working together will bring you fame and fortune, so, as they say, don't believe your own press.

Another consideration when crafting your vision: own your uniqueness. What differentiates you from others? Don't be afraid of what sets you apart. Did the birthmark hurt Mikhail Gorbachev? An image consultant might have said, "I don't know if people are going to buy the guy with the big wine spill on his head." But Gorbachev owned what he had, and while people might have noticed that mark, what they noticed most was the mark he left on the world.

Along the same lines, newscaster Bree Walker was born with a genetic condition called ectrodactyly, a deformation of her fingers and toes. She owned that. She didn't become a big deal *in spite of* her condition; she became a big deal—one of the highest paid local TV news anchors in the nation—*because of* the articulate, courageous way she dealt with it.

Most people want to sweep uncomfortable truths about themselves under the rug. But when you don't own your uniqueness, everyone is going to focus on it and it will obscure the message that you seek to present. I mentioned earlier the blonde TV host who feared that she was interchangeable. You do not want to be interchangeable in today's world.

So create your vision now. Make it realistic, definable, believable, and summarize it in a single sentence. This vision will become your road map for going forward. It can sound something like this: "I'm going to be . . . a senator who listens to the people," or "an actor who makes great choices and doesn't sell out just to get a role," or "an environmentalist who makes a difference."

Is crafting a vision that simple? Indeed it is. The next step, creating your messages, is at the heart of the next chapter.

CHAPTER 5

THE KEY TO SUCCESS: GETTING YOUR MESSAGES OUT

Now you have a vision of the future you want to create and share with the world. The media is the filter for sharing that message, so the question that this chapter will answer is how best to communicate what you want to say through the appropriate media and to the audiences you wish to reach.

Since the media is the conduit, we have to use media-friendly tools to make our points. The most media-friendly tool of all is what I call *messages*. And the best messages of all are those that make your points quickly, effectively, and clearly. In the Internet age, there's no time to dawdle when you're communicating your thoughts to the world. A million years ago—okay, thirty years ago—when I started out, a sound bite on local or national news lasted fifteen to twenty seconds. Those days are gone. Sound bites shrank first to under ten seconds and then to today's few well-chosen (we hope) words.

If you want to see just how much the world has changed, rent a movie from twenty or thirty years ago or watch a sitcom from the seventies or eighties. The scenes seem interminable compared to the quick cuts employed today in everything from

TV news and sports to movies and music videos. So you've got to be quick about saying what you need to say, and I'm going to show you how to do that.

One thing that has not changed is the ability of human beings to absorb information. No matter how fast technology gets, the human brain is still capable of absorbing only three or four pieces of information or messages at any one time. If you're fortunate enough to get your story into a newspaper or on TV—and even if they're doing a big profile on you—you'll likely have the chance to make only three, four, or five points.

Most newspapers are written and edited on a junior high school level, so you don't really want to be overly complex. Your initial job is to excite your audience enough to want to sample whatever it is you're talking about. An actor appearing in a new movie wants people to buy tickets to the film. Companies launching a new product want consumers to try it. Even if you're a nuclear physicist, you've got to talk to people at a level they can understand and not make your message too complicated. Conversely, though, you don't want to treat people as if they're stupid. It's not that people cannot handle complex information; it's just that if you're too hard to understand, they'll tune you out. And it doesn't matter who you are.

"Dr. Einstein," reporters once asked, "you've come up with this new theory of relativity. What does it mean?" Albert Einstein was far too smart to give them the same complex explanation he would have given others in his field. Instead, he told them. "Put your hand on a hot stove for a minute, and it seems like an hour. Sit with a pretty girl for an hour, and it seems like a minute. *That's* relativity."

We don't have to be Albert Einstein to understand that great messages are simple, easily absorbed, and appropriate for their audiences.

When I think back to high school, where Miss Windsor taught me the basics of journalism, I recall the five W's: who, what, when, where, and why. These questions are also the foundation of good PR. In fact, journalism and public relations are necessarily symbiotic, since the goal of press agentry is to get people and events into the media. So if you want to make a journalist's job easy, and if you want your message to be disseminated clearly to your public, focus on those questions. There's really no need for much more than that.

Another journalistic precept that comes into play here is the inverted pyramid: the important information goes first. You can always elaborate later—in a subsequent interview, on your Web site, in your advertising, or in other forms of marketing. But when you're using the media to get your message out, make sure you stress the important points when you're doing an interview. I always tell my clients to respect the interview process, the interviewer, and the questions, but really work hard to get the most important information out there first. So let's take a look at each of these questions in turn.

Who are you? That's the first message you've got to create. Let's say you're an actor who has done a new film and is now promoting that film through interviews with the media. An experienced actor well-known to the public has little to explain. George Clooney doesn't have to tell us much about who he is. We know already. But a young actor in his or her first major motion picture would invest a little more time in the "who" question, explaining where she grew up, how she got into acting, and what other projects she might have appeared in before this one.

I'll relate all of these concepts to non-Hollywood settings in a moment, but let's keep up with the movie theme as we move to the second question: "what." What's the movie? What's the TV show? What's the thing that you're promoting? You can always tell a message-trained actor or actress when Letterman or Leno asks the fateful question, "So tell me about this movie."

The untrained actor will say, "Well, there's a girl, and she's in school, and she meets this guy . . . but she's not really dating the guy . . . she's, like, dating his brother . . . but she kinda likes the guy, but she splits up with the brother and goes to college. . . ."

By now Leno or Letterman is slumped over the desk, and the

answer is still going on. Twelve years later, the actor winds up his spiel, the show goes to commercial, and the producer is making a mental note never to have that person back.

It's a pet peeve of mine when I see someone describing a movie in those terms. The point here is that the "what" message has to be relatively succinct. Try this instead: "It's the story of a couple who meet in high school, where they're a little flirtatious, and they get together later in life and find what true love is really about." That's a great "what" message; you nailed it within the bounds of the modern sound bite—just a few seconds.

You don't have to be a rocket scientist to know that if you're going to be in a movie, you'll be asked what it's about. (You don't have to be a rocket scientist to become an actor either, but that's another story.) So be ready to describe who you are and what you're trying to accomplish.

Let's take the same subject and put it into a different context. You're the president of the PTA and you're trying to get a recycling center opened at your school. Who are you? What's a great way to summarize the "who" message? How about: "I'm Jane Smith, a local resident and a mother of three. I've been president of the PTA at my children's school for the past three years."

Perfect—so let's move on to the what. What exactly are you trying to accomplish? "One day, I was parking behind the school and I saw dumpsters overflowing with bottles and paper and other things that really should be recycled. I got together with some other concerned people and helped design a recycling station for our community."

You couldn't have possibly nailed the "who" and "what" questions any better. So now let's move on to the third question—"when." When is the movie opening? What's the next deadline for your recycling facility? Putting a date into a story does a number of great things. It gives a sense of time perspective, and in media terms, that's a hook. It adds a sense of urgency: something has to happen by a certain time, so we've all got to get moving. And adding a date clarifies your strategic goals from now until the time your movie opens or your event is to take place. To what date would we tie the recycling plant story? Perhaps to the day the school board is to vote on it. Or the date by which you must have enough signatures on a petition to get it approved.

What would a "when" message sound like in this context? "We're asking everyone in the community to call or e-mail the school board to express support for the recycling center before their meeting next Thursday night." Boom. In one sentence, you've put a time stamp on your message, and you've delivered a sense of immediacy that will catapult your listeners into action.

Now on to the fourth question—"where." This is just simple geography. If it's a movie that's going to open in 3,000 theaters across the country, that's all the actor on Leno or Letterman needs to say: it's coming soon to a theater near you—or better, coming Friday to a theater near you. If a film is going to open only in limited release, and if we were doing an interview with a Los Angeles media outlet, we'd say, "It's opening Friday at the Sunset 5." Specificity is good.

What's the "where" message for the recycling station? "It's going to be in the old storeroom behind the gym, which hasn't been used in years." Or, "It'll be at the dump three miles outside of town." Specific, to the point, simple, and clear.

Who's really great at getting a message out? Don't roll your eyes, but I'd have to put Richard Simmons at the top of the chart. He will never go on TV unless he has a reason to do so. And he'll tell you exactly what he's doing; it might be Deal-A-Meal or a new TV show, and he may look hokey and you may laugh at him, but he sure can get his message out. You don't have to wear spandex tank tops and shorts to succeed in your own media campaign, but you do have to be clever and authentic.

If you're looking for a little more elegance and polish, tune in to the Sunday morning political shows. Most politicians are pretty darn good at getting their messages out. They understand that one of the main points of media training is to stay focused on a specific idea and to not veer far from it, regardless of where the interviewer wants to take the conversation. Another individual who is really good at getting messages out is Donald Trump. You may not like him or his style, but if he's on with Regis and Kelly and pushing *The Apprentice* or a new book or an appearance, you'll know exactly what messages he's trying to get across. Similarly, Ricki Lake is a really good guest on talk shows. She only goes on when she looks great, is prepared, and knows exactly what she's promoting. When she's there, she's ready. She always has a great story and knows her messages. I would put Keith Olbermann in the same league. When he makes a point, you know exactly what it is.

The converse is to let glibness get in the way of messages. It's terrific to be funny, but don't let your need to seek approval through humor impede your messages from getting out. Similarly, when politicians equivocate (a fancy word for flip-flopping), they look bad. Same thing in Hollywood—you just end up getting both sides mad at you. Don't be afraid to take a stand and defend it.

We've now covered the who, the what, the where, and the when; that leaves us with the "why." It's essential to explain why you're doing something, because the world no longer takes anything on faith. In a cynical society like ours, you've got to be specific if you want to be credible. It's not enough for an actor to say, "I am in love with . . ." Instead, if the public is going to believe him, he's got to give some reasons. "I love her because she captured my heart—she's intelligent, strong, beautiful, and she challenges me to grow." That's something even a cynical audience will understand.

Let's face it—sometimes we do things just for the money. But you'll never hear an actor say that. Instead, the actor will say, "I took this role because it challenged me, and the film really expresses my values." That actor might be snickering all the way to the bank after the interview, but that's Hollywood. I'm more impressed when an actress like Sally Field is straightforward when she is interviewed about a new TV show in which she plays someone her age—a woman in her sixties. Instead of avoiding that role like the plague, which is what most actors and actresses her age would do, Sally delivers a "why" message that reads clearly: "I'm proud of my age and my battle scars. That's why I'm playing the role of a woman in her sixties." And that's a "why" that piques my interest.

Why are phone companies getting into the Internet business? What's the "why" message they put out to explain that business move? "We're not in the phone business," they'll say. "We're in the communications business, and we need to embrace communications no matter how they take place." Let's go back to Jane Smith and her recycling facility. When the reporter asks, "Why are you starting this recycling facility?"—and the reporter *will* ask that question—Jane had better be prepared with a really good answer. Here's the answer I would suggest: "Because even in this small community, we create two tons of waste a day. At the end of the year the waste we create in this town would fill our football stadium up to the thirty-eighth row." A visual reference always helps. Make a note that facts and statistics help in the "why" part. And you don't have to have a hundred statistics—just one or two really telling points will get the job done.

What if there's controversy surrounding the project, idea, or product you seek to promote? Think back to the film *Brokeback Mountain*. If you're an actor in that film, you can't avoid talking about the "gay thing," so it's something you should be prepared to address. The interviewer is inevitably going to ask, "Why did you pick this role?" You've got to be able to say, "As an actor I wanted the chance to be part of a great love story that is so powerful our audiences might just forget their prejudices and reach a new level of enlightenment."

Who could argue with that? Okay, a lot of people, but that's beside the point. My point to you here is that the "why" question is vital, and the interviewer will ask it, so be ready for it.

There's a sixth question that sometimes arises—the "how" part. If you invented something or improved something, inquiring minds will want to know how the thing works and how you did it. For example, there are now programs on cell phones that allow the phone to finish a word that you start typing. What's the advantage of that? It's clear—it's going to save you time, and perhaps keep you from spraining your thumbs. So the interviewer is likely to ask how the program works, because it's a pretty cool thing. The company might explain, "We went through eight million sentences and had them broken down by a computer algorithm. We discovered that when you type in these two letters in the context of a sentence, 99 percent of the time this other letter is going to follow."

A client of ours called ComScore.com keeps track of Internet use the same way Nielsen provides ratings for TV shows. ComScore.com gets in the news every year over the holiday season, for its predictions of Internet use, of what's hot on the Internet, and so on. Why do we believe them? Because they explain their "how." They have access to millions of people and computers and are therefore able to make accurate predictions. Similarly, film director Robert Zemeckis, who has given the world *Roger Rabbit, Forrest Gump, The Polar Express,* and *Beowulf,* among other great pictures, is known for having a technological advancement in every one of his films. The natural media question: "Bob, how did you make that film look so good?" So, if your topic involves technology of any sort, you'll get the "how" question. Be ready for it.

I keep telling you to be ready. How exactly do you do that? My suggestions: Write down what you have to say, and practice with people. Talk to your family and friends. Tell them what you're doing in the same small number of words that you would use in an interview. That way, when you go to the media to be interviewed, it won't be the first time you'll be speaking those words. In fact, by the time you get to the interview, your ideas should sound fairly refined.

The trick is to sound spontaneous even though you've prepared these ideas long in advance. Truly, the best "spontaneous" moments are the ones you prepare for. Think back to Lloyd Bentsen's repost in his vice presidential debate with Dan Quayle, when he said, "Senator, I served with Jack Kennedy; I knew Jack

Kennedy; Jack Kennedy was a friend of mine. Senator, you're no Jack Kennedy." It looked to all the world as if Bentsen had become incensed by Quayle comparing himself to JFK during the debate. In fact, Bentsen and his handlers knew that Quayle was likely to make that comparison, since he had done so many times before, and the JFK–Dan Quayle chasm was something that they had been seeking to exploit throughout the campaign. Bentsen had that "You're no JFK" piece prepared and ready to roll out, and it was just a question of waiting for the right moment to do so.

How do you know if you've got a good message? Here are the tests:

1. *It's simple*—accessible without being patronizing. You never want to be perceived as patronizing, unless you're talking to kindergartners.

2. *It's appropriate.* In other words, you're the right messenger for the message. A 400-pound doctor with a diet book may want to think about hiring a spokesperson. But if a doctor who weighed 400 pounds gets down to 185 pounds, his diet book will have more credibility than someone who has weighed 185 his whole life. We used to represent 7-Eleven, which had an individual on its team specializing in reducing the number of robberies of stores. What gave him his credibility? He used to stick up 7-- Elevens, had gone to jail, and had changed his ways. Who knew better about stopping bad guys than a bad guy who had switched sides? (Both the diet doctor who drops 200 pounds and the reformed criminal doing store protection are also reminders that we do love turnarounds—we love it when people take something bad and turn it into something good. So if that's part of your story, stress it.)

The biggest mistake you can make is to have overly long or complex messages, things that are just too hard to understand. You can always start with something simple and build on it later, but you cannot start with something complicated and work your way back to simple. You can also blow it by talking about issues other than the project you are there to promote. I've seen actors talk about politics and their love lives but fail to mention the film they're there to talk about in the first place.

You've got to get your messages right, rehearse them, be authentic, look right (we'll get into that later) . . . and then you'll be ready to meet the media. If you're on *Larry King Live* for an hour, terrific—you can go deeper into your story. But otherwise, just keep to those basic messages: the "who," the "what," the "when," the "where," the "why," and, if appropriate, the "how."

One final point: if you're launching a business, a Web site, an idea, a movie, or anything else, make sure everyone on your team is on the same page so that one consistent message goes out. If you don't tell your own people how to talk about what you're doing, they'll talk about it in their own terms, and you'll end up with inconsistent messaging.

We recently worked with a high-end residential real estate company just starting out in a very bad real estate market. We approached all the people associated with the new company on how to respond if anyone asked, "What are you, crazy? Launching a real estate company in a market like this?" They all had the same "here's why" answer, and this united front worked wonders at delivering a clear message. So getting the right message out is important not just for you but for everyone associated with you. And as you're about to find out, there are more people in your life than you can imagine.

CHAPTER 6

YOUR TARGET AUDIENCE IS LISTENING

W e've said throughout this book that PR today stands for perception and reality, but when we talk about the original concept of PR, public relations, we need to look at the first half and one of the most important factors in the equation—the public. In reality there are multiple publics, because we all don't have the same publics, and we generally have more than one. This chapter discusses how to identify all of the different publics that will be receptive to your message. Once we figure that out, we can think about how best to address each of these audiences. But for now, let's concentrate on the issue of identifying the publics—the different audiences for the messages you need to get out.

Perhaps the best example of success in identifying target audiences that I've seen in a long time was Nancy Pelosi's ascension to the position of Speaker of the House of Representatives. She is the first woman in American history to earn that title. Take a look at what the *New York Times* had to say on January 2, 2007, about how thoughtfully Speaker Pelosi identified her various constituencies and audiences—her multiple publics, if you will:

> In the three-day stretch of whirlwind events beginning on Wednesday, Mrs. Pelosi will celebrate her heritage (at the Italian Embassy), her faith (in a Roman Catholic mass), her education (at Trinity College), her childhood (in Baltimore) and her current home (in a tribute by the singer Tony Bennett of "I Left My Heart in San Francisco" fame).
>
> She will embrace her status as the first female House Speaker with a tea for women. She will highlight her pull among Democrats with a thousand-dollar-per-person fundraising concert. And she will welcome visitors to the halls of Congress in an open-house tour.

That's a brilliant example of defining and appealing to target audiences. Let's say you're Speaker Pelosi. How would you create a media list to speak to each of these audiences? You're Italian, which means that you can go to Italian-language publications in the United States and also English-language publications aimed at the Italian community. Your story is of international scope, so you can go overseas to all the newspapers, magazines, and TV and radio stations in Italy, should you so choose. Many of them have news bureaus in Washington, D.C. As a Roman Catholic, you can target Catholic publications around the United States and around the world. Closer to home, you can include all the church bulletins and newsletters in San Francisco on your media list. These outlets, which can easily be overlooked, actually provide a fantastic pipeline to the individuals who can reelect you to office every two years. And don't forget the broad category of women's fiction.

Next comes education. You can have articles appear in your college newspaper, alumni magazine, the newspaper in the town where you attended college, and other similar publications. Then there's your childhood. You grew up in Baltimore, which brings Maryland newspapers into play. And the "hometown" angle crosses over into Washington, D.C.—isn't that convenient?

You see how the game works. You consider all of the various constituencies, audiences, and publics who might be receptive to your message, and then you include as many as you possibly can to get your story out in the widest possible way.

Depending on the publication, you'll want to shape any articles accordingly. Let's say that we wanted to soften your image for whatever reason. My first thought would be to get a picture of Tony Bennett serenading you in the pages of *People* magazine. If this were my mission, I would have you sitting and looking schoolgirl-esque as a smiling Bennett croons to you. I would bring my own photographer, so that I would be certain of the quality of the results, and I would tell him exactly what I wanted. I would be certain to hire a *People*-caliber photographer and not the guy who does weddings and baby pictures down the street. Or I might invite *People* to cover the event, and offer special access or an exclusive story. Once the photographs were taken, I could look at the shots instantly, either at the location of the shoot or in the comfort of my office or home. Digital cameras today can send photos wirelessly and instantaneously over the Web. No more getting up the next morning to look at contact sheets with a magnifying glass. It's routine to edit a shot while the shoot is still going on.

Of the twelve best shots, I would crop the right one, and make sure it was the right resolution for reproduction in a magazine. Of course, I would have gotten *People* onboard first, to ascertain that they had some level of interest before I went to the trouble of putting all this together. But that's how the game works. You may not need a *People*-level photographer for a local event, but you certainly want to make sure that you've contacted the media outlets on your list and let them know what you have in mind.

The juxtaposition of Speaker Pelosi and singer Bennett symbolizes the crossover between politics and entertainment. The *Los Angeles Times* actually has a very talented reporter—Tina Daunt—whose beat is the intersection of Hollywood and politicians. She might be a good person to contact for a story about how San Francisco entertainers all came out for Nancy Pelosi. If I can get three to five decent celebrities onboard, I might invite *Entertainment Tonight, Extra, Access Hollywood,* or *E! Entertainment* or other such shows. That way, I've got the entertainment media dialed in.

Last but not least is the political media. Since this is a national story, I would have everyone in the Washington media on my list, from C-SPAN to the morning talk shows, from Fox News and CNN to the most important bloggers. And then we swing back to San Francisco, which has a huge depth of media—two daily newspapers, local TV stations, community newspapers, newspapers in outlying communities, bloggers, radio stations, and so on. With a media plan like this, I would have hundreds of potential media outlets onboard prior to her swearing in.

Today, the media is more interconnected than ever. A handful of corporations own most of the leading media outlets, and those that do not share ownership cross-fertilize each other (and I use the term fertilize deliberately) with syndicated stories. Once your story starts appearing one place, it gathers steam—or legs, as we in the PR industry say—and begins to appear elsewhere as well. But whether you are working with a local newspaper circulating to 5,000 people or the *Los Angeles Times,* you should treat every media outlet the same way. Everybody wants to feel important—that's one of the most fundamental lessons I can pass along.

One of the major differences between publicity and advertising is that you pay for advertising, which means you want to target your audience with as little waste as possible. Waste is money spent that does not return buyers. For example, if you were running for city council in Santa Monica, it would be a waste to buy an ad reaching the whole country on the NBC *Nightly News.* But, if the *Nightly News* did a news story on you (publicity), thousands of people in your district would talk about it and it would generate a great deal of buzz.

In public relations, a little waste is okay. It's just as easy to make a phone call to the *New York Times* as it is to the *Flint Journal*. Excess circulation won't hurt you. With PR, a shotgun approach is usually acceptable.

But no matter where you're getting your message out, be sure that your most important stakeholders hear it from you first—before it hits the media. If you've got a new product, a new service, or an important change in your business, don't forget to tell your employees first. Employees, shareholders, and the like are hugely important publics. Treat them as such. People hate reading things in the newspaper before they hear it from the boss. From a legal standpoint, if the information will have "material" effect on the stock price or the future of your company, you don't want rumors floating around. When the article does appear—and most newspapers are printed the night before they hit the streets, or appear online—you could e-mail your employees the story right away, so they don't find out something important about their company only from the newspaper. People just hate that. You've got to define your own watercooler conversation, or others will define it for you, perhaps in ways you don't like.

When the Writers Guild of America went on strike against the Hollywood studios and producers in 2008, it was intriguing to see to whom the two sides were talking. The writers took their case to the court of public opinion, so they communicated with mass market entities like the *Los Angeles Times* and the major TV networks. They went on YouTube.com. Did they really care about influencing the way everyone in America thought about the strike? Not really. In fact, most people didn't think about the strike at all. Unless your livelihood is directly affected by what goes on in Hollywood, the strike was something of a nonissue. But members of the Writers Guild read the *L.A. Times*, so it was a great way to get information out. Plus, they wanted to tell the public that they would not be seeing their favorite television shows. They wanted to blame the producers—claiming their turf first.

The Writers Guild doesn't care much about what the public

thinks, but it certainly cares about what their members think. This is an illustration of the fact that a little bit of publicity overkill isn't going to hurt. If you get the public onboard with you, so much the better. By contrast, the studios went to the *Wall Street Journal*, the Business sections of major newspapers, MSNBC, and CNBC. Their message: "Our company can handle this. Our stock will do just fine." Same strike, different message, totally different publics.

Now let's talk about you. Let's say you're an attorney running for state representative. What influences which outlets go on your media list?

> ➤ The city where you grew up.
> ➤ The city where you live.
> ➤ Where you went to school for your undergraduate work.
> ➤ Where you went to law school.
> ➤ Your religious affiliation.
> ➤ Your political affiliation—left, center, or right.
> ➤ Causes in which you're involved.
> ➤ Where your wife grew up.
> ➤ Where your kids go to school.

It's not just "How do I get the local paper to write about me?" The real question is "What are all the different places that would be interested in doing a story about me, helping me get my messages out?"

Let's talk more about causes. If you're that lawyer running for state rep, ask yourself what issues and causes you support the most. Let's say that you believe we're not tough enough on crime. Seek out anticrime groups that would applaud your call for tougher sentences. Look for relevant and influential blogs and speak to them and offer to write opinion pieces. There is a wealth of opportunities in the media through which you can get your messages out, at practically no cost to you. It's certainly a lot cheaper than making a hard-dollar advertising purchase. Think carefully about all of the different publics interested in what you have to offer. You will be shocked at how large a group you can aggregate.

Sometimes you can get more than one story in the same paper. One of my clients opened a fine arts and wine warehouse—basically storage lockers for the moneyed class—in West Los Angeles. There are enough people who live in Los Angeles only part of the year, or who are away for extended periods of time, to make a business like this economically feasible. We placed not one but three stories in the *Los Angeles Times*—a story in the Business section, a story in the Westside section, and a story in the Food section. This was possible because with big newspapers, there is often less coordination and communication among the various sections. A tiny paper in a smaller town is more likely to limit the number of times you can get your story in. Whether you can get one story or multiple stories, though, leave no media outlet unturned. After all, your publics await.

CHAPTER 7

GETTING THE GOODS

What kinds of materials do you need to get your message out to the world? In the past, a press kit, a photo, and a brochure got the job done. In the Internet era, everything has changed. You need your own Web site. You probably need to be on MySpace.com and Facebook.com. How about some videos on YouTube.com of your successful speeches, awards, or other great moments? And what about a video clip that can be viewed on or downloaded from your Web site or handed out to people as a DVD?

In a previous chapter we talked about the messages that you want to deliver. Now we're talking about the methods by which you deliver those messages. As we all know, those methods have radically changed in the last ten years. Your messages, however, are the driving force behind your PR campaign. Now it's time to think about an aesthetic—a look, a feel, an overall gestalt, if you will, for all of your materials so that there is a consistency in the manner by which you deliver your message.

Nothing drives me crazier—and I'm hardly alone on this— than mismatched materials. If the design of your business card varies radically from that of your Web site, which looks nothing like your stationery, which has no design elements in common with any brochure you might have, we have a problem. Just as you have to put out the same message on a consistent basis, so your materials must be consistent. This is the time to take a look at everything you're putting out that has your name on it and ask, "Are all of these materials reinforcing the same messages . . . and reinforcing them the same way?" As I tell my clients, I don't even care if you choose the wrong point of view. Just choose one point of view, because the first key to successful materials is consistency.

I had a client who was the CEO of a company. He said, "The products should be the stars, not the CEO." He didn't even want people to know what he looked like. He mistakenly thought that if someone took a picture of him, he owned that picture, since he was in it. I explained to him that while they couldn't use a photo of him in an ad, they could own it, and display it in their home, or put it in a news story. He went on a very expensive campaign, found virtually every journalist who had photographed him, and bought out the photos so that they would never appear anywhere.

We have established that our messages must be delivered in a consistent fashion through all of the materials we create, and that the materials need present us and our image in an authentic way. So how do you go about creating really great materials that serve these purposes?

I always tell my clients to take the pulse of other people's Web sites as they begin to develop their own. Be sure to look at the Web sites of your competitors and rivals, but also of people not in your field. Get design ideas. What do you like and dislike? You can compare the process to remodeling your home, or designing a home for the first time. Often, the best way to start that process is to grab a bunch of design magazines and start tearing out pages of things that you like and don't like, so that you can give your designer or decorator an idea of your taste. Make a list of all the design elements and functional features that you see on other people's Web sites so that you can include them on your own.

Let's say you're a realtor and you are creating a new Web site for yourself. Visit other realtors' sites and you'll discover that one has a link to the Multiple Listing Service, offering clients the convenience of seeing all available listings on the realtor's Web site, while another realtor has a page of family photos, which humanizes him and separates him from the pack by showing him as a family man. Another site has a mortgage calculator. And another has a resource guide telling you how to find the best roofer in town, the best handyman, and other helpful information and advice. Get a sense of all the things that you would like to include on your Web site by browsing what is out there.

I've learned almost everything I know about establishing an effective presence on the Web from my friend and mentor Larry Weber. Larry began his own PR company in the late '80s and within a decade it became one of the world's largest PR firms. He is currently the chairman for Digital Influence Group, a social media marketing agency. As a world-renowned expert in marketing and public relations, Larry tells us there are four types of sites to be viewed as placement opportunities on the Internet. First are the reputation aggregators, like Google and Yahoo. Second are the blogs, the bastion of "citizen journalists." Third are e-communities, which may be iVillage.com, AskMen.com, or People.com. And the fourth are social networking sites like MySpace.com and Facebook.com, which are quickly becoming the most important.

But the real centerpiece of your message delivery system, if you will, is your own Web site. I hear it all day long—people saying, "I don't need a Web site." Or "I don't know how to put a Web site together." Frankly, people are intimidated by the concept, which is ironic, because there are tons of ten-year-olds who have their own Web sites. My goddaughter, Eve, got her own Web site when she was born. It was easier and cheaper for her parents to put her pictures up there than to mail them to everyone in the family.

So if babies and ten-year-olds can have Web sites, why not you? It's much easier than you think. Most service providers—Earthlink, Yahoo, Google—will give you free space for a Web site. They'll also give you templates for Web sites, so that you can create your own. Whether you're a chiropractor, a horse trainer, or a candidate for public office, you'll find beautiful templates that will help you create a Web site from scratch. Can you develop an extraordinary, compelling, one-in-a-million Web site using the starter kits from your service provider? Probably not. Is it a great start? A place to claim some real estate on the Web? Absolutely.

If you're still wondering what a Web site can do for you, let me give you the example of a doctor, an internist, who uses his Web site to great effect. The first thing you see when you go to DrCohan.com is "First Class Care." Because it's Dr. Gary Cohan's Web site, he gets to define himself instead of being lumped into a broad category of general practitioners. There's a welcome message, and you can even schedule appointments online. You don't even have to call the office and wait on hold for ten minutes only to discover that the person with the appointment book is out to lunch. You can schedule an appointment online at three in the morning in the blink of an eye. That's a good thing.

He also has a page on emergency preparedness—information he wants you to have to make your life better. He's got a life-expectancy calculator, diet tips, cholesterol information. Safe-sex guidelines. A page on how to quit smoking. Links to the Web pages of other specialists he likes, should that be necessary for you. You may not need all of this, but you can only come away from a Web site like that thinking to yourself, "Damn. He's thorough." You might still make your appointment the old-fashioned way, and you might never bother with any of his essays, links, or other doodads and trinkets on his site. But you certainly come away having received a very strong message—and I emphasize the word "message"—about his professionalism and how much he cares about the lives of his patients. That's a critically important message for a doctor—or for anyone—to deliver, especially in the "service economy" era, where, ironically, good service seems to be a thing of the past.

Let's take another doctor, who performs laser eye surgery. When you go to his office, they sit you down and have you watch a video for ten minutes that explains the process of how the surgery works, what it does for you, any risks, the recovery process, what you can expect, and so on. Having you watch a video in the office is a big step up from the doctor explaining the same thing over and over again to one patient after the next. But now the doctor has put that video on the Web, which means that you can watch it in the comfort and privacy of your own home instead of having to sit in his office.

Anything that saves you time or makes your life more convenient is a good thing, and it also demonstrates the kind of person the doctor is. He doesn't just care about you and your eyesight. He cares about your time. He wants to make everything as easy as possible for you. No more sitting around the office waiting for somebody to get the video player to work right. It's all in your hands. He also has on his Web site a list of frequently asked questions, which saves both him and you time.

A Web site is not just an investment in message delivery. It's also an excellent investment in time management—and in this meshugge world of ours, who doesn't want to save time? Whether you create your Web site from a template, or whether you bring in a computer whiz and spend a few hundred to a few thousand dollars to get your site up, there are certain commonalities to successful Web sites, so let's take a look at them now.

Typically, your first page offers a welcome and an overview. You want some kind of mission statement on that home page, but don't just sit down and write your mission statement out of thin air. We've already gone to the trouble of taking the pulse of your community—however you define your community—about who you are and how you are perceived, and you've already gone to the trouble of creating messages about how you *want* to be perceived. Your current image and the image you want to create should form a cohesive whole with your mission statement.

You certainly want a biography of yourself on your site, but you don't want to create the same kind of resumé that you would offer a prospective employer. Nobody cares that you were a summer camp counselor twenty-three years ago. Instead, this is a document with a purpose—you want to shape (not lie about) your biography so that people have the best possible indication of who you are, what you've done, and what you offer. Even in this era of transparency, you don't have to put everything on your Web site, from the time you ran a red light and got a ticket to the fight you had with your neighbor. But you must be truthful, or you will get nailed. We've seen over and over people who have exaggerated their credentials and are then challenged and even publicly humiliated. Just because you're reaching for something more doesn't mean you have to claim you are more than you are right now.

Your Web site must be easy to navigate. Again, go to other people's Web sites, talk with your friends, and, most important, talk with young people. What makes a Web site attractive? What makes it well organized and easy to get around? Impatience is the hallmark of the Internet age, so if your Web site doesn't measure up to acceptable standards—and those are constantly changing—people will not stick around to figure out who you are or what you have to say.

If you're offering a consumer product, then you want to present information about that product. Keep it simple—here's this new product and this is what it does. Let's say you're opening a dry cleaning business. In and of itself, that's not newsworthy. But let's say you're opening a "green" dry cleaning service that does not use chemicals harmful to clothing and the environment. *That's* newsworthy. Let people read all about it and get caught up in the excitement of what you are offering. You can put in a history of dry cleaning and your place in that history, as long as what you write is engaging and interesting.

What about photography? Definitely include photography, but make it appropriate and authentic. President Reagan, thanks to his image consultant Michael Deaver, was the master of the well-placed "photo op." When a politician is launching a campaign, the town square of his (or her) hometown is the perfect backdrop. Or if you are starting an environmental campaign, you might kick it off—and pose for a photo or video for your Web site—in front of an environmental mess you're trying to clean up, or, conversely, in front of an environmentally healthy and beautiful place that you're trying to create. Your images need to match your message.

We live in a world where image and video are extremely important. If you can put a short credible video on your Web site, do it.

In the video age, facts often take second place to feelings. I'm not saying that it's ever acceptable to lie or stretch the truth on a Web site. I am saying that the impression you leave is often more important than the facts you use to build your case. In moments like these, I think back to the movie *JFK*. That film had a lot of factual mistakes in it, but it was hard to leave the movie theater and not believe that there was some sort of conspiracy and cover-up about Kennedy's assassination. Obviously, you're trying to create a much more positive feeling in the minds of the people who visit your site. What feeling are they receiving as they look at your photos and video?

How many photos should you have? Not too many. What does it tell you about a person who has too many pictures of herself? An ego run amok? Is that the image you want to create for yourself? Doubtful, unless you are a supermodel. A few tasteful photos are really the best way to go. If you're the PTA president, you should be standing with a classroom of smiling kids. If you're a state rep, you should be posing in front of your state capitol. If your family isn't too bad looking, put them on the Web as well.

Back in the old days—okay, ten years ago—the press kit was the cornerstone of a media campaign. A press kit consisted of a group of materials gathered in an eight-and-a-half by eleven-inch folder to be sent out to the media. Today, I mostly discourage the printing of press materials. The exception is when you have a media event planned and you want to be able to hand things out to members of the media that day. In this case, you can't tell them "It's all online." You've got to hand them something. Today that often includes a DVD. But by and large, the press kit is a relic and not something on which you want to invest too much effort, money, or time.

Why am I down on press kits? First, information changes quickly. If you get an award the day after you've printed your press kit, you've got to reprint it. Same thing if you move your office. It is costly and it's not good for the environment. Some old-line journalists still like getting things in the mail, but they are becoming increasingly rare. Instead, your Web site ought to be your online virtual press kit. That way, people can find what they need on the site and print those pages out instead of having to wade through a lot of material that has nothing to do with the story they're trying to write.

Delivering your messages over the Internet is also much less expensive—good-bye FedEx charges, not to mention the cost of employees putting those packages together. If a reporter for the *New York Times* calls me and requests material for a particular story, I just e-mail him or her the link, and we're done.

There are times when beautiful paper embedded with elegant flecks, and an elegantly embossed name and address at the top, makes a difference. If you're selling luxury goods—diamonds, a $10 million house, high-end skin care—sometimes your material *is* your message. You can't tell customers at a luxury jewelry store to "Go online and see our stuff." Printed materials can make a difference. But in a declining real estate market, for example, there's nothing worse than a beautifully printed brochure for an expensive house with the price repeatedly crossed out and lowered. That totally destroys the image of elegance that you're trying to create.

Leeza Gibbons has an image book that is one of the most beautiful things I've ever seen. It's somewhere between a brochure and a press kit. It positions her with the causes and products with which she is aligned. You look at it and it says, "This is a classy lady." There are times when it's worth making that kind of splash.

So, on your Web site, you want to create a "media" or "news" section that serves as your online press kit. You might have a news release about yourself: "Jane Rogers Announces Campaign to Run for State Senate." You might post additional stories about yourself as the campaign continues. Whatever you're doing, offer a history or a time line, so that people can understand where your current activities fit into the overall scheme of things. Make the photos on your site easily downloadable so that journalists can take them and put them into their own Web sites or into newspapers or magazines.

Not everyone visiting your site has to have access to your press kit. Take the example of television networks. In the old days, every journalist covering television would receive an individually printed press kit from the network. Today, of course, it's a different world. If you're a journalist covering TV, you apply for a password to access secure portions of the networks' Web sites. NBC doesn't want the general public accessing a lot of this information directly. It figures that the public doesn't need to know who the producer of a given TV show might be. As a result, only accredited journalists have access to information that the networks deem inappropriate for the general public.

You can do the same thing on your site—have a password-protected area just for the media, or just for your donors, or just for other parents in your daughter's second-grade class. And so on. This approach saves thousands of hours and tens of thousands of dollars in terms of organizing, printing, and delivery costs.

What else do you put in the news section of your Web site? Clippings of articles in which you've been featured, copies of speeches, editorials you've written, whether they've been published or not. If you're a political candidate, position papers. If you do post clippings from magazines and newspapers, make sure they are done neatly and beautifully. It shouldn't look as though your five-year-old kid cut the story out of the paper with the round-headed scissors. Also make sure that you indicate where the article was published and when it appeared. My own personal pet peeve is articles from publications that are no longer in business or that have changed their graphics. Nothing makes a Web site—and its subject—look more dated and irrelevant.

What if there's some nasty stuff in an otherwise positive article? Pull a quote or a couple of paragraphs from the article. You can't edit all the nasty stuff without running into potential legal problems, so I'd be very careful about that. Links are hugely important. Offer links on your site to people, places, causes, and issues that will be useful to your visitors. A dentist might link to the American Dental Association, or to an article on painless dentistry from a medical journal, or to a particular toothpaste brand that he likes (or that he is sponsored by), or to a top-ranked dental school. He might even include a study on which toothpaste or toothbrush is the best. This is his chance to define himself not just as a dentist but as a trusted adviser to his potential patients.

What else? Videos or DVDs are essential. It's relatively easy to create your own video today. Dress appropriately and authentically and have your video scripted in accordance with your messages. Don't make it painfully long. Anything over three minutes and you'll start to lose people. Podcasts are an important feature of many Web sites today, in which you give a lecture or talk about your subject. You can make these long or you can break them out into five-minute segments, and people can download them to their iPods or other listening devices. Many people like to listen to information while driving to work or jogging. Some people like music, and others like to learn things. It's not a value judgment—it's just another opportunity for you to reach out to your marketplace.

We have something in Hollywood called electronic press kits, or EPKs. These are fed to broadcast journalists and Web sites around the world so the actors, directors, and producers can save the time and effort of doing hundreds of interviews. An example is the "How the movie was made" section added as a bonus feature on many film DVDs. They typically involve interviews with stars and the director, asking them questions like "What attracted you to this picture?"

If you wrote a book and you want to sell it, include a link to Amazon.com, bn.com, Borders.com, or any other place where people can easily purchase it. If you've created a product, offer links that allow people to buy the product or a link to stores that carry the product.

One of the masters of online marketing is the comedian "Larry the Cable Guy." He makes a ton of money selling merchandise at concerts and online with his "Git-R-Done" trademark expression. Take a look at his site and you'll understand just how lucrative the world of online merchandising can be.

If you're a celebrity, you can have a place on your site where people can request an autograph. I think it's a little tacky to sell your autograph unless the money goes to a good cause. So make sure that the cause is relevant and authentic to who you are. Daisy Fuentes's mother is a breast cancer survivor, so it would make sense for her to be creating a connection between herself and that cause online. If you're an athlete, you could charge three dollars for your autograph with the clear understanding that the money will go to support a Boys Club or YMCA. Again, it's got to be something authentic to you.

Everybody says that people hate advertising, but the reverse may be true in some cases. Think about all the people who watch the Super Bowl just for the advertisements. If you have a company famous for creative and entertaining advertising, why not make all of those ads available as a library on your Web site? You already paid for all that creative work; why not continue to get mileage out of it? Stylish furniture designer Mitchell Gold ran a very clever, award-winning ad campaign that featured his bulldog. On his site, you can find links to all those ads through the years. It never hurts to remind people of why they liked you so much in the first place.

It's essential to have a contact page so that you can make it as easy as possible for people to get in touch with you; you don't want people to feel as though they're wandering in the wilderness trying to track you down. It costs almost nothing to create an e-mail address that makes sense for you. I don't know how many times I've received resumés from people who use the same goofy e-mail address in their work lives that they do in their personal lives. Am I really going to hire goofyguy33069@aol.com? Or sexychick55599@earthlink.net? It makes sense to have different e-mail addresses for the different aspects of your life, and it makes complete sense to have an e-mail address for yourself on your Web site consistent with the image you are presenting to the world.

I suggest obtaining the following separate e-mail addresses: (1) a personal e-mail for family and friends; (2) a business e-mail for professional correspondence that includes some variation of your name; and (3) a commerce e-mail. This is the e-mail you use for financial transactions on the Web—for eBay, online banking, shopping, etc. This way, if you get an e-mail to any address other than that regarding commerce, you'll know it's a scam. You can have additional e-mail addresses for your volunteer work, parenting, and the abundance of e-mails you receive from schools, clubs, and anything else relevant to your life. E-mail accounts can be created for free. Don't be stingy with yourself.

Along those lines, when we receive resumés from people who want to work at our agency, we look them up on Facebook .com and MySpace.com, just to see what they're saying about themselves. One guy who actually got a job with us depicted himself mooning someone on his MySpace.com page. Probably not the wisest career move to have that thing up there; you never know who's looking at your world.

If you are running a political campaign, make it easy for people to send a donation or buy merchandise to support your cause. When Barbara Boxer was first running for the U.S. Senate, she sold "Boxer shorts" as a cute fund-raising tool. She was in a crowded field and relatively unknown and this was a great way for people to remember her name. Larry the Cable Guy offers "Git-R-Done" thongs. Boxers, thongs—yes, they're both undergarments, but there are some not-so-subtle differences between the two. Whatever you're offering has to be "on message," or else we have trouble on our hands. Also, let people register easily on your Web site to be on your mailing list or to get newsletters, but make it easy for them to "unsubscribe." Nothing upsets people more than getting spam when they don't want it.

Many years ago a friend of mine was running for city council in West Hollywood, California. It is between Los Angeles and Beverly Hills and has a huge gay population. Under the guise of dirty political tricks, his opponent sent out thousands of photos of the candidate's nude photo spread from a gay magazine many years earlier. My friend won by a landslide. Know your audience.

We've talked a lot about creating your own Web site, but that's hardly the only thing to do on the Internet. Let's explore some other options as well. Let's say that when you Google yourself, you don't like a lot of the stories that come up. Here's something fascinating you might not have known: you can actually pay people to bury those things in the Google results. There are algorithms that certain computer experts employ to change the order of items that come up in the course of a Google search.

This process doesn't make bad things go away, it just buries them farther down the list. Chances are, if you search on Google or any other search engine, you'll only look at items on the first or maybe the second page, but rarely will you go any further than that. If there's something really snarky about you on the Web, whether true or false, wouldn't it be great if suddenly that article or story could be dropped down to the tenth or fifteenth page? Well, it can, for a price. Again, it doesn't make bad stories go away—it's more like covering up a blemish with makeup. It might be below the surface, but at least it isn't visible to the naked eye.

The reverse process is called Web optimization. This means that the same techie who buried your bad stories also has the ability to bring good stories about you—or your Web site—to the top of the search entries about you and your area of expertise. For example, you can ensure that if people search "realtor Los Angeles," you come up at or near the top of the list. How do they do this? They use algorithms or mathematical computer programs that search for your name or business, say, seventeen million times. Suddenly, the computers over at Google think to themselves, "Damn. He's popular." And up you go to the top of the list.

How does Google feel about being manipulated in this manner? Not so great. They've got their *own* techies playing a cat and mouse game with the search optimizers, trying to keep those sudden seventeen-million-hit searches from affecting their placements. So you can't just do this one time and consider it done forever. You've got to keep your Web optimization person close by, because your number one or number two ranking could always change at the drop of a hat.

With regard to the Internet, I want to counsel you to be proactive instead of reactive in all things. Take Wikipedia, the grassroots encyclopedia that happens to come up at or near the top of practically every Google search these days. Wikipedia is hugely popular, free, and often wildly inaccurate. Anyone can register with www.Wikipedia.org and create or change the Wikipedia page about *you*. Unless you're truly controversial, no one is likely to mess with your page, but they could. If you don't have your own Wikipedia page, be proactive and put one up about yourself. But be careful: if you put lies in, you'll get nailed and your credibility will plummet. Word will get out there that you lied on your Wikipedia page, a cyberspace faux pas if there ever was one. And once you put your Wikipedia page up, visit it frequently to make sure that no one has tampered with it. The more controversial you or your issue might be, the more often you should check to make sure that things are as they should be in Wikipedialand.

Let's talk about Facebook.com, since everyone else is. Facebook.com is a hugely popular social networking site. When most adults think of Facebook.com, to the extent they think about it at all, they think of teenagers spending endless hours glued to the screen, creating fanciful Internet identities for themselves and sending and receiving countless instant messages to and from their friends. All that is indeed going on, but Facebook.com is also being used aggressively these days as a marketing tool.

Whether you are a realtor, an actress, a singer, or an attorney, look at the Facebook.com pages of other people in your field and create something that feels right for you. Social networking sites really are one of the most dynamic and explosive technological developments of the Internet era, and you've either got to get onboard or be left behind. On Facebook.com, Myspace.com, or any other social networking site, you can define yourself by categories and interests and connect with like-minded people. Since it costs nothing to join, it's a heck of a lot cheaper than an ad in the *New York Times*.

FaceBook.com, which started off as a more elite social networking site for Ivy League students and alumni, now has a broader audience. There's also ASmallWorld.com, which targets an upscale audience. There are social networking sites for specific groups—Jews, Irish Catholics, Mormons, and gays. Do some research and find out which of these smaller networking sites might be right for you and your messages.

Then there's LinkedIn, which is a social networking site for professionals. I probably receive eleven requests a day from people on LinkedIn to be my "buddy." Unless it's John Wayne Gacy offering me an invitation, I'll say yes. You can't have enough friends.

Like a Web site, the page you create for yourself on practically any social networking site can be very sophisticated. You can upload photos, video, music, spoken word, practically whatever you can think of, and you can change them almost instantly whenever you want. What's the point of going on MySpace.com? Again, it's a way of controlling the means by which your message gets out to the world.

Take Owen Wilson. After his suicide attempt in 2007, he did his "big catharsis" interview not with Barbara Walters or in front of a news conference, where others would be able to control or edit his message. Instead, he did an "interview" with Wes Anderson, the director of his new film, on MySpace.com. They ignored the personal issues entirely and just focused on the fact that he was back making and promoting movies. Eventually, when Owen does an interview with a real journalist, he may have to deal with those issues, but for now, he's bought some time. As a result, the producers of his film are able to focus on the marketing of the movie, not on the emotional stability of their star.

YouTube.com is also another phenomenon of the Internet age. It won't be long before more people are watching videos on YouTube.com and similar sites than they are watching traditional over-the-air television. Put yourself up on YouTube.com—anything that you're proud of ought to be there. Obviously, pay attention to the legalities of copyright law, because you don't want to buy trouble.

People in my profession are also using YouTube in a similar way to MySpace. After his high-profile divorce announcement from Star Jones, my client Al Reynolds chose to do his own interviews on YouTube instead of the traditional media.

Never be afraid to hire professionals to review your Web site, but don't forget to talk to friends and see what they think. I always recommend publishing a site for friends first—let them take a look at the site, offer their comments on the overall look and feel, let you know if they spot any typos, and just make sure the thing does what you want it to do. Get feedback for a few weeks. It's better to hear about a mistake from your sister-in-law, or to learn from someone in your office that a link doesn't work, than to have the same thing written about you in the *New York Times.*

If you're doing a Web site, try not to have pop-ups from commercial entities, even if you can make money doing so or they offer you free hosting. These things are distracting. Don't make your Web site hypercommercial, where it's all about sales—of your stuff or someone else's. You can have tasteful Web hosting without any outside advertising for a very small amount of money, so there's no reason to cheapen or diminish your message by saving a few dollars in this manner.

At the beginning of the chapter, I used the word "gestalt" to describe the overall look and feel of your materials. If you take the suggestions I've offered in this chapter, you will have created for yourself a Web site consistent in look and feel with the rest of your marketing materials—your letterhead, your business card, and any brochures that you print from time to time. At the same time, you've used Web optimization to push your Web site to the top of the list and to bury any negatives about you that might be hanging out in cyberspace.

You've created or updated your own Wikipedia page, on YouTube you've uploaded positive videos about yourself that are "on message," and you've created appropriate pages for yourself on MySpace, FaceBook, LinkedIn, and other appropriate social networking venues. Each one of these tools is working harmoniously with the rest to create the message you want. It's a little like the marching band at halftime. Each member of the band is playing his or her instrument, marching in a particular pattern, all getting together to make that big M. The band is playing "The Victors" and they're marching down the stadium as the University of Michigan football team has taken a commanding lead. (Okay, I'm a Michigan guy. Pick your own band.) The main thing is that you want all of the methods by which you get out your messages to be marching consistently and cohesively, without any off-notes, so that the messages you seek to deliver are getting across loud and clear to the constituency you're seeking to influence. That's what good PR is all about.

CHAPTER 8

THE DEATH OF THE TRADITIONAL PARTY,

OR WHY CIRQUE DU SOLEIL PERFORMED AT JASON'S BAR MITZVAH

What would the Oscars be without the after-parties? What would the presidential inauguration be without the series of gala balls across the nation's capital? And what would a five-year-old's birthday be without friends, a birthday cake, and pin the tail on the donkey? Or, in Hollywood, a performance by Beyoncé? Everybody loves events. So what's the difference between a party and an event? We throw a party to celebrate something, or to just get friends together and have a good time. By contrast, an event is an opportunity to get a message out. And that's why events are staples in the world of PR. In this chapter, I want to share with you the approach to event planning that the entertainment industry and major corporations use, and I'll show you how to adapt these same approaches to your own marketing campaign.

First, let's ask why you would want to consider going to the expense and trouble of putting on an event in the first place. Here are some reasons:

1. *It's what we call a "publicizable moment."* This means that you can get media attention before, during, and after your event, garnering for your message repeated exposure to the constituencies you want to hear it.

2. *It's a great way to introduce people to something.* If you're offering a new product or a new service, or you're moving to a new office, or you've got a cause or a charity to promote, an event is a great way to focus the attention of everyone in your community on your offering.

3. *It's a great way to get people together.* When you've got all of your supporters under one roof, you create extraordinary opportunities for networking, synergies, and empowerment. Perhaps the people who feel the same way you do about your cause have been under the mistaken impression that they are toiling alone. When you bring them all together, they get energized simply from the sight of so many other people who believe in the same mission or cause.

4. *Events motivate people.* An attractively and appropriately produced event gets a buy-in from people who become your volunteers, board members, donors, sponsors, or supporters. An event shows that you're serious about your cause, and that you are willing to put in the time and effort it takes to get it on the map. A solid event committee will live on and do good work long after the event is over.

5. *It's a public platform for you.* It's an opportunity for you to tell the world what you have done . . . and what you want to do. If you engage the media properly—and we'll talk about how to do that—you can focus enormous attention on your goals.

6. *You can raise money.* There's nothing like a well-produced event to motivate people to get out their checkbooks. Practically anything that we want to accomplish in the world takes money, and demonstrating effectively and sincerely the value of your mission is a great way to tell your story to potential donors.

7. *It's an opportunity to honor people.* Why do so many fund-raising events honor particular individuals, whether they are donors, celebrities, or individuals who have demonstrated a long-term commitment to a cause? It's not just because they buy a lot of tables for their friends. It's because people like to be honored and respected for the hard work they have done. It's only natural. A high-profile honoree is also newsworthy, so this is a great way for you to recognize people for what they have done and also get news of that recognition (and your cause) out to the world.

If any of these reasons appeal to you, and I expect that a number of them will, then you can see how an event can be an important part of your PR plan. So how do they do things in Hollywood? Almost every event, whether it revolves around the opening of a new film or the support of a good cause, includes these three basic elements: a celebrity, a sponsor, and a cause. I call them the golden troika of branding. Why do you want a celebrity? To attract attention. Why do you want a sponsor, or many sponsors? So you don't have to pay for it. And why do you want a good cause associated with the event? To put a halo over the whole thing; to make it more than simply a bunch of people getting together to have a good time (not that there's anything wrong with that).

Hollywood is often accused of doing things in an "over the top" fashion, and that's true—I did go to a mogul's grandson's bar mitzvah where Cirque du Soleil performed. People, however, are getting a little more careful about how they spend money. Not too long ago, movie studios still spent a lot of money on premieres. Remember the film *George of the Jungle*? It was a big Disney remake of the cartoon show and starred Brendan Fraser. The premiere wasn't just a red carpet in front of a big theater in Westwood. Instead, all invited got to take the train from Los Angeles down to San Diego at Disney's expense, where they had a picnic and tour of the Wild Animal Park, followed by an outdoor screening of the movie.

It was a fun event, and everybody had a good time. In reality, though, Disney may have gotten no more attention or publicity for the train ride to San Diego and the Wild Animal Park visit than if they had simply conducted a screening at the Motion Picture Academy in Beverly Hills. All the TV crews want is to talk to the stars, and they could have accomplished that in half an hour on Wilshire Boulevard instead of trooping all the way down to San Diego. If you don't have the budget of a movie studio, you want to ensure that your event does not become overkill.

Today, in fact, all but the biggest movies tend to have perfunctory parties, and the galas are the exception and not the rule.

The opposite is true as well. It seems as though everything in the media world has gotten bigger, faster, and stronger, and even seven-year-olds have come to expect a clown or a princess or some other performer at their birthday parties, not just the traditional games you and I played when we were kids. Maybe that's just how it is in Hollywood, where people book Stevie Wonder or the Beach Boys for sweet-sixteen parties. Whatever you do—however you find the "sweet spot" that's not too big and not too small for your purposes—the main thing is that the event must be authentic to and connected with whatever you are trying to promote.

The best example I can offer in this regard is Oxfam, the international organization that seeks to alleviate hunger in poor and war-torn countries. When you entered the Oxfam dinner, you got a chip, and depending on the color of the chip, you might be served the complete, full-on dinner that you would enjoy at a typical high-end restaurant in the United States, but if you drew a different color chip, you would receive the more simple, subsistence-level meal that someone would be eating in one of the countries that Oxfam serves. Often this meant you'd sit on the floor with nothing but a meager bowl of rice balanced on your knees, and as you watched other diners sitting at their tables with their fancy china and sizzling steaks, the concept of world hunger became more real and visceral than it had ever been before. The point of all this is that all elements of the event have to be consistent with the message you wish to send . . . or you're just dancing in the dark.

Gatherings don't have to be huge to be classified as events. Let's say that you are an attorney, and you want to become a partner in your firm. An "event" could be as simple as inviting the managing partner to lunch to discuss your position in the firm, or hosting a dinner party for six or eight at your home, or taking a group of the decision makers out for an evening. Even an event that involves only you and one other person requires planning, care, and thought. If it's going to be a one-on-one, don't leave it to your lunch partner to tell you where to make plans. Instead, you choose the restaurant, and make it the most appropriate place in town.

Let the setting demonstrate to the managing partner exactly the kind of person you are and exactly the kind of social settings in which you function best. If you're not sure where to go, you might call the managing partner's executive assistant for suggestions on where the boss likes to eat. Everybody loves it when you come with a plan instead of a vague idea about getting together: "Paul, I'd like to have a conversation with you about my future here with the firm, and since this is a matter of considerable importance to me, I'd like to propose that I take you to lunch at Orso." Paul will not fail to be impressed.

Let's say there is a slightly larger group of decision makers whom you must influence. A dinner party at your home is a very effective way to bring them together and focus them on the question of your advancement. Yes, this does mean that you, or your spouse, must cook dinner . . . although you can certainly have it catered if cooking a fine meal is not something you feel comfortable doing. Again, keep in mind that the difference between a party and an event is that an event is simply a party with a purpose. Everything that happens, from the invitations your guests receive to the evening itself, must reinforce the notion that you want them to absorb: that, for example, you truly are partnership material.

I'm not suggesting that you can become partner in a law firm just by throwing a good dinner party. But it doesn't hurt. So much of business is social, and while the people at work may be familiar with your work product, they may not know anything at all about your ability to function in the sort of social gatherings that would involve clients and prospects for the firm. Showcase those skills in an appropriate way. An alternative to a dinner party would be dinner and a night out at a game. Practically every city has either a professional or college sports team. Here in L.A., it would be dinner at the Palm followed by the Lakers at the Staples Center. But wherever you are, there's a great restaurant and a game. Again, choose the best place in town for the reasons we mentioned a moment earlier and get great seats. (If you're not in L.A. and you're paying for the tickets, count your blessings.) It's a small but wise investment in your career.

Let's talk about invitations in greater detail. Today, it's common to invite people to parties through the use of Evite or other online invitation Web sites. The problem is that people don't always pay attention to their e-mail, and an invitation could easily be overlooked. Similarly—and with all due respect to our friends at the post office—things do get lost. Though the postal service never seems to lose the bills, we can't always count on it to deliver invitations to people who are of critical importance to us in our lives or our careers. This is one area where you can take matters into your own hands . . . literally. There's nothing like a handwritten and hand-delivered invitation to make the event—and the invited guest—feel very important. A company in Los Angeles called Creative Intelligence actually creates handmade, highly elegant invitations that cost hundreds of dollars each. If you got an invitation like that, would you even think about missing the party?

When we were talking earlier about creating materials, we emphasized that everything should have the same look and feel. The same is true of an event; the invitation must convey the same feeling as the event itself. Use your judgment wisely in this regard, and you will have people anticipating your event and allowing nothing to interfere with it. Also, be aggressive yet polite about following up on your invites.

Let's move on to a slightly larger event. Say you're the head of the PTA and you want to do a really extraordinary fund-raiser for your school. There's already one major fund-raiser for public schools—called taxes. But it never seems that enough tax dollars trickle down to individual classrooms. So parents have to take up the slack. The question becomes How do you mold that Hollywood trinity of cause, celebrity, and sponsor into a local school event?

Let's first talk about sponsors. You can probably find dozens of them. The easiest way to find businesses that will sponsor an event to support a school would be to look on the back of your kid's Little League uniform. The same businesses that sponsor local sports teams, from Little League to Pop Warner, also take out ads in the yearbook and contribute in other ways to reach parents and families in their communities. Approach them and offer them something unique. There's nothing worse than simply having your logo among a dozen other logos, each in its little square, on the back of a T-shirt. I mean, who cares? Who are you going to influence with something like that? Instead, invite Joe's Auto Body to sponsor the school's go-kart track—and then they can offer a special on dent repair. Have a local restaurant provide the pies for the pie toss; the poor souls who get a face full of pie might be so impressed that they place an order for ten coconut creams. You get the point. Give each sponsor something special and authentic.

So now you've got sponsors, which means you've got the money to put the event on. You've also got a great cause: the school. So where do you find a celebrity? How about the principal? Wouldn't it be fun to have the principal on the plank going into the dunk tank? What about the mayor or another local elected official? What about a newscaster or radio personality from your area? In all markets, radio and TV stations are always looking for community activities to support. It's great marketing and advertising for them, and it's also part of their legal mandate for using the public airwaves. A local TV station sponsor can do a live remote, and they can list your event in the community listings on their Web site. At the event, a TV or radio station can pass out free stuff from their van—mugs, hats, or whatever they've got going on. It always adds a level of excitement when the media arrives. Media can provide not just attention for your event but also sponsorship, and sometimes even the celebrity around whom media planning for the event can take place.

For a moment, let's think about taking the celebrity aspect of the equation up a notch. Can you fly in a Hollywood star to preside over your event and gain extra media attention? You bet. Practically any Hollywood star can be had ... for a price. The minimum to get in the door with a major celebrity is two first-class plane tickets, limo pickup at the airport, a suite at a decent hotel, and—for a female celebrity—hair and makeup. It might also cost a speaker's fee, or a charitable donation. Be respectful of any celebrity you bring to town—be nice, don't ask a lot, and you'll get much more than you bargained for. There's no putting them up at Uncle Lester's house, and don't recount in full your experiences in vaudeville sixty years ago as a way to compare your own dramatic talents.

At the event, make everything easy and clear for both your celebrities and the media. Make sure your celebrity guests feel special at all times; give them an escort so they can easily find where they're supposed to go, cater to their needs (as long as they aren't off the wall), and generally give them a red (or a green, if it's an environment-related event) carpet experience. Give your photographer a "shot list" and let him know exactly whom he is to be shooting and against what backdrops, if that is relevant. I try not to let celebrities hold alcohol or cigarettes in photographs, unless the party is sponsored by a liquor company. I'll never forget one memorable event at which I went to hold the drink of an aged Hollywood legend. I said, "Let me hold that for you while we take this photo." She grabbed her glass back and screamed, "That's my drink." I loved it, realizing it was an authentic moment for her.

Make it easy for media outlets to get the video they need. Take advantage of the fact that your event will give you promotion at three different times: when you're announcing it, while it's happening, and afterward, when you send out photos and video to relevant media outlets and supporters. And take advantage of the fact that you've got all these willing hands present. Have sign-up lists handy so that people can volunteer for things. Make it easy for people to donate money. Make it easy for people to do whatever you want them to do. Above all, make sure everybody has a good time.

How do you get celebrities? First, figure out which celebrities are tied to your cause. My client, Ricki Lake, flew around the world, often at her own expense, promoting midwifery and home births because this is a cause in which she deeply believes. Do a little homework on the Internet and see who supports what; it's more likely that you will find a celebrity willing to visit your part of the world if the agenda of your event matches up with his or her interests. How can you contact them? Try a Web site called WhoRepresents.com, where, for a fee, you can type in the celebrity name and find that person's agent, manager, attorney, and publicist.

The Screen Actors Guild as well as the Association of Talent Agencies offer similar services for free. IMDB.com (Internet Movie Data Base) has a paid database. If you want the celebrity to attend without a fee attached, call the publicist. If you're intending to pay a fee, go through the agent. What do celebrities cost? That number is a function of their current standing in the public eye and is subject to negotiation. If you aim for a B-level celebrity, you'll still have someone who adds a lot of glamour and excitement to the festivities, but you won't have to go through all the hassles that bringing in an A level person can often entail. Your cause can easily be overshadowed or even upstaged by the mad chase between the A-level star and the paparazzi. Don't let your message fall victim to that circumstance.

Now let's talk about a larger-scale event. You're getting a

ballroom in a hotel, and you've got important people coming in. You've got a lot of work to do. I always advise people to start on the smaller side, and have a successful smaller first event than flop on a large (read: expensive and publicly embarrassing) scale. The best Hollywood events started off small and grew to grand proportions. It's better to have an overstuffed smaller room initially than a half-empty larger room. One feels like success and the other feels like a bit of a disaster.

I'd like to tell you about an event that might give you a few ideas, especially if you are thinking about anything to do with the environment. The environment is, if not *the* biggest, one of the biggest causes and subjects of discussion today, cutting across all lines of business issues. Architects, designers, and engineers are building ecofriendly houses, stores, and office buildings. Companies are creating everything from clothing to heating ducts out of environmentally friendly, sustainable materials. The whole world is going green. So how do you get word about your commitment to the environment, whether you are driven by philanthropic or business needs, to the world at large?

Here's how a builder in Southern California did just that. He designed and built a $3 million home in Venice, California, a trendy section of Greater Los Angeles, and everything from the ground up was environmentally friendly and sustainable. But how did he cut through the clutter of the Los Angeles real estate market to sell the place? He brought us in to promote his project and create an event for the house. It actually consisted of three weekends during which people could come and view this striking new ecofriendly home.

Let's go back to our checklist. Cause? The environment—we benefited a great charity called HealthyChild.com. That's a winner, especially in today's world. Sponsors? All that you could think of, and more. Ford Motor Company was a sponsor; the house came with a Ford Escape hybrid SUV in the garage. If you own a house like that, you've got to have a hybrid, right? It was a great way for Ford to associate itself with an ecofriendly story.

Other sponsors included clothing companies that make clothing out of sustainable materials, the architect and designer, and many other business entities connected to the environment or seeking to align themselves with this extremely cutting-edge cause. Celebrities? We had tons of A-list names, because the environment is the first choice of causes for many Hollywood celebrities.

So who came? Over three weekends, three thousand people visited the house, each paying twenty dollars, from which a portion went to support local environmental groups and HealthyChild.com. And you can be sure that all of this attention focused on the house called attention to it when similarly priced houses were sitting on the market month after month.

What can we learn from this intriguing example of celebrities, sponsors, and cause all working in alignment?

➤ *Be creative* and don't limit yourself in terms of who you think could sponsor your event, whether you're focusing on the environment or something entirely different.

➤ *Think big.* While it's true that the corporate offices for Ford might be located nowhere near your locale, there's a Ford dealer somewhere in the neighborhood, and wouldn't they like to get on your bandwagon if there's a legitimate tie between Ford products and what you're offering? If you were repeating this idea of an environmentally friendly home being built in your community, I'd recommend you go to the largest appliance dealer in town. That dealer—and GE, which makes ecofriendly appliances—would be a natural sponsor for the events.

➤ *Make it fun.* Who wouldn't want to see an environmentally friendly $3 million home? It's a great opportunity for people to get some ideas about their own homes or just simply enjoy the practice of lookie-looking . . . at a fairly high price point. By the way, everybody had a great time.

➤ *Be respectful of your attendees' time.* There were no four-hour seminars on how to build an ecofriendly house. Instead, people could be in and out in a half-hour or less if they so chose. There's nothing worse than an event that drags on for hours, with endless speeches and PowerPoint presentations. People just don't have the patience, and you'll risk alienating the very people whose support you seek. Keep things brief, and you'll make more friends.

I would be remiss if I did not mention the key elements for any party: good lighting (warmer colors make people look healthier); a good sound system that *you* check ahead of time (you don't want it to sound like announcements from a sound truck in North Korea); and good food—lots of it. If you run out, so will your guests. Or, as my grandmother believed, "If there wasn't more left over than you consumed, you didn't have enough food." Another thing about food—if you're having a full dinner, let the guests know. If it's just desserts, tell them. If they know what to expect, your guests will be happier.

Finally, maintain a comfortable temperature. If it's an outdoor event and it becomes cool, have space heaters available or wraps for the ladies. A hot auditorium will only become hotter when thousands of people stream in. Start out cooler than you need indoors—it will warm up. I was always taught that each person gives off the heat of a 200-watt lightbulb.

There's nothing like an event to create excitement, media attention, and that all-too-overused expression, "buzz," for what you're building. Whether it's ascending up the career ladder, saving the earth, or anything in between, the well-planned event is an important part of anyone's PR arsenal.

CHAPTER 9

MEDIA TRAINING: PREPARING TO FEED THE BEAST

In this chapter, we're going to talk about undressing for the media. You can keep your clothes on because we're talking about a *mental* undressing—in which you share your ideas with the world in media interviews: television, radio, Internet, and print. There isn't a single serious political candidate, business leader, movie star, top athlete, or other celebrity who would dream of appearing in the media in any form or fashion without proper media training. In this chapter, I will share with you the media training that I provide my celebrity clients, and show you how to use that same training in your world.

Most people don't like doing interviews. It's right up there with public speaking in the minds of many. I'll ask, "How'd the interview go?" They'll respond as if they were the goalie for a hockey team; if they didn't get their teeth smashed out, and if the other team didn't score, that's a good interview.

That's absolutely the wrong paradigm. That's a defensive paradigm. When you do interviews, play offense. The biggest mistake people make when thinking about interviews is that they have no objective measures for how the interviews should go.

We do media training for three basic reasons. First, we want to make people who aren't very good at interviews decent enough to get by. Second, we want to make people who are "good interviews" even better. And third, we want to train our clients to handle sensitive topics or specific issues so they feel empowered and confident.

An interview is an opportunity for you to broadcast to the world those three to five points you developed in chapter 5. A great interview is one where you look your best, appear relaxed and confident, come across as honest and articulate—funny, perhaps, but definitely not glib—and told great anecdotes that support the messages you're trying to get across. That's a successful interview. I want to show you exactly how to make that happen.

Why does it matter? Why is it necessary to deal with the media? Keep in mind what I've been saying from the beginning: half of your job is getting your work done; the other half is getting your messages out about the work that you're doing. This means that you always want to ask yourself, Why am I doing this interview? Do I have something I'm selling? An idea I'm promoting? Is there some other reason? Or are there good reasons for me to not do an interview right now? What you say in an interview can and will be used against you in a court of law. So if you've got a sensitive legal matter going on, lay low unless there's a very good reason for doing media. Don't say anything that could come back to bite you later on. And don't do an interview if you would be betraying confidences or risking someone's life. As I write these words, there is a kidnapping of children in the news right now. Anyone who has serious information about that situation ought to be communicating it privately to law enforcement, not talking about it on *Nancy Grace*. Just because you *can* get press doesn't mean you should get press.

A perfect example of this is Heather Mills, the ex-wife of former Beatle Paul McCartney. Their marriage ended and she was trying to get her reputation back. She went on *Dancing with the Stars*, which was a good image move, but then she started doing media interviews. Big mistake. Why? Because she didn't give any news in those interviews. She said things like, "If people knew the real reason we divorced, they'd stop hating me." The overriding message she was trying to present was, "There's more to this story than just Paul's side," and "I'm not a fortune hunter—this is just a marriage that didn't work out, and we would rather not talk about why." The problem was that since she had no specific information to offer, her hysterics became the story, and she ended up looking worse than if she had never gotten in front of the camera. It's that old story—it's tough to claim that the media is invading your privacy when you're the one who's doing the interview.

So we're going to assume that you've got a legitimate reason to do interviews. After all, that's the premise of this whole book—that you're reaching for something more in life, that you want to take your career or some aspect of your lifestyle to the next level—and part of that process is getting the word out to the people you need to influence. It's vital to know how to prepare for interviews and what to do once the cameras or tape recorders are rolling or the reporter has his or her pad and pencil out.

When I conduct professional media training, my starting point is to ask my clients what they think the media really is. My older clients—those over forty-five in particular—have some pretty highfalutin notions about the media. Older people generally hold the media in higher esteem than do younger people. Those of us over the age of—well, never mind—remember the time when TV news and newspapers were held to a high standard of ethics. In the Walter Cronkite/Chet Huntley/David Brinkley era, if you knew what side of a story a journalist stood on, he was a bad journalist. Now you know where the whole network stands. In other words, the whole question of objectivity is pretty much out the window these days. Things have changed. That old model, in which the media is a respected part of society, is gone.

Today, everybody treats the media for what it is—a business, just like Hershey's chocolate or Coca-Cola. They've got a product, and they want people to buy it. The more people who watch, listen, or read, the more they can charge. The only difference is that we're guaranteed freedom of speech, not freedom of Diet Coke, but there's still an idealistic part of me that wants to respect the media. The reality is that they're putting you on TV or on the radio or in their newspaper or magazine because they think you are going to draw eyeballs. And guess what? You're doing the same thing.

There has always been a symbiotic relationship between journalists and PR people. Years ago, the *Washington Post* made the announcement that they would no longer talk to PR folks like myself. That rule disappeared after just a few months. Journalists need us PR folks—or they wouldn't have enough to write about nor know how to navigate the waters of our clients. The other side of the coin is symbolized by a writer for the technology magazine *Wired*, who complained that he was getting 300 story pitches a day in his e-mail. Sorry, pal. It goes with the territory.

Now you understand your relationship with the media, but what are you supposed to say in an interview? Three things: messages, bridges, and anecdotes. First, your message points—the three to five points we discussed earlier supporting your proposition. You're a city councilman running for state rep, you're the PTA president running for the school board, you're a local environmentalist trying to effect change in your community. But you've got to get your messages out so that you don't sound as if all you're trying to do is . . . get your messages out. You never want to look rote or mechanical, as if you were reading from a script. Ideally, you want to come across in a way that paints you as charming, warm, and funny. You want to seem as though you're telling the interviewer everything he or she wants to know. In reality, you want to stick to your three to five messages as much as possible.

I believe an interview is a great place to telegraph information. True stories abound of actors who said they would like to host a talk show or do a great romantic comedy. Guess what happens? People in powerful places read the interview and say, "She would make a great talk show host." So if you want it—telegraph it.

The second thing you want to do in an interview is called *bridging.* When the interviewer tries to take you to an area where you're not comfortable, to get you to talk about something you don't want to talk about, the bridge is what takes you back to your message. For example, a journalist asks, "Mr. President, are you concerned about the new data from the Federal Reserve showing the economy is slipping even further?" That may not be a question the president wants to answer. So he can bridge by saying, "Yes, that data is a concern to me, which makes it even more important than ever that Congress passes my budget as quickly as possible so that the American people get all the services they need."

What did the president do there? He acknowledged the point, but he quickly bridged back to one of the messages that he wanted to get out. A bridge is different from a dead end, which is where you end up if you don't have the ability to segue back to your agenda instead of following that of the reporter. It's very important that you have your bridges handy, because the media is not there to serve merely as an amplifier for you. The outlets have their agenda, which is to present many sides of the question, not just yours.

You should never be surprised by what they ask or what they know about you. Assume that the media can and will pull up absolutely everything about you that exists on the Internet or in other research venues. We talked about how political campaigns do opposition research not just on the opposition but on their own candidates. If you've done your own homework, you know what's out there, and you won't be surprised by a question designed to throw you for a loop.

Let me give you an example. A few years ago, a major fight broke out at a Detroit Pistons game. One of the spectators who was involved in the fight appeared on *Good Morning America* the next day. He went on wearing jeans, a baseball cap, and a sweatshirt, which I thought was a very wrong choice. It was disrespectful to the media, and people feel that. He looked like a guy in his thirties who thought he was still a cool kid in his teens.

Sorry, pal, you didn't look cool. You looked goofy and smug. He answered the questions, but then Charles Gibson threw a curve ball.

"This isn't your first trouble with the law, is it?"

The guy went pale. If he'd been smart, he would have known that researchers at ABC News would take the five minutes necessary to pull up his criminal record. And there, for all the world to see, was the fact that he had been involved in an incident in the past. Don't let this happen to you. I'm not talking about getting into fights in basketball arenas; I'm talking about getting into a media interview where you find yourself surprised by the fact that they have pulled something up about you on Google, on YouTube, in a book, or anywhere else. And this doesn't apply just to national media. If you're interviewed by a local TV or radio outlet or a local newspaper or magazine, you can end up looking just as foolish in your community as a major celebrity can appear on a nationwide basis. It's just not worth the trouble.

So far we've covered getting your messages out and bridging back to them when appropriate. Now let's talk about timing and anecdotes. Let's say it's an hour-long interview and it takes ten minutes to get your messages taken care of and another five to bridge. So what do you do with the other forty-five minutes? Your message points are essentially the skeleton for your interview, just the same as the outline and table of contents serves as the skeleton for this book. What you fill in along the way are anecdotes that buttress your points in the most effective fashion.

For my money, the most brilliant spinner of anecdotes in our times was the late president Ronald Reagan. Like Barack Obama, I didn't agree with Reagan politically, but I respected his ability to get his message out and inspire people to vote against their own self-interest. It didn't even matter if his anecdotes were true. What mattered was that Reagan felt them so deeply that he was able to convey his messages to the nation in ways that seemed heartfelt and genuine.

Many politicians have learned the lessons of the Great Communicator, and they understand that it's more effective to tell a story or present an anecdote than to simply make assertions or provide statistics. For example, contrast these two approaches to a question about health care. Politician A spews numbers and statistics about the health-care crisis in America. Politician B says, "When I was in Iowa, I met a farmer who had gotten sick, and since he couldn't work, he had to choose between paying for food for his family or for his own medicine. If I'm elected, we will not leave the middle class behind." Isn't that anecdote—short, powerful, to the point—far more effective than a litany of statistics?

If you're going to spend so much time sharing anecdotes in your interviews, it makes a lot of sense to decide in advance what anecdotes you are going to tell. And then rehearse them—in mock interviews with your friends or coworkers. Record yourself on audio so you get a sense of what you sound like. Record yourself on video so you can see yourself telling the stories. But above all, don't expect to come to an interview ready to wing it. This isn't amateur night at the Improv. This is your golden opportunity to get your messages out there. So be prepared.

Typically, when I'm working with an actor who has just finished filming a movie, I'll have him develop the anecdotes that he'll use when promoting the film. I'll ask him things like, "Tell me about the first time you read the script," or, "What was it like to work with that other actor?" or, "Tell me about the character you played." This is a great way to generate anecdotes that can be used in an off-the-cuff, spontaneous manner during interviews. Okay, that actor might be telling those same anecdotes to forty different interviewers over the course of a single day, but at least he's prepared. He knows where he's going to go.

If there's a controversial scene in a movie, we'll be certain to discuss that. For example, when I was doing media training for the two lead actors in *Brokeback Mountain*, we all knew that "the kiss" would be a highly controversial moment, so they had to come prepared to talk about that situation. For the *Brokeback* team, it was talking about the film and what it achieved and why; it was talking about each person's journey to this project, and the understanding that it was a truly collaborative effort that just wouldn't have been the same if the stars had not aligned in just the right way. In the end they should be exquisitely proud of everything the film achieved in terms of filmmaking, financially, and, most important, in opening some people's minds. To have had even a slight association with *Brokeback Mountain* is something I regard as one of the great honors of my career.

After you've listed your anecdotes, rehearse them. Keep in mind that they have to support your messages in a clear, understandable way. They cannot be long, drawn out, or boring. A few sentences gets it done, just like that politician I mentioned a moment ago who talked about the farmer he (allegedly) met in Iowa. And being self-deprecating is always good. If you're the butt of a joke, people won't be laughing at you by mistake.

Larry Lyttle, a legendary Hollywood television executive, discovered Judge Judy, and as his company's publicist, I worked with Judge Judy at the NATPE (National Association of Television Programming Executives) convention in Las Vegas. This is where executives from local television stations around the country get together to choose the syndicated programs they're going to air in their hometowns, and where the celebrities from shows available for syndication go to make their case. Judge Judy is a pretty confident gal, and after she did her first interview, she turned to me and said, "So, how did I do?" She was expecting me to praise her, but I was getting paid to tell her the truth.

"Uh, fair," I said, and saw she was shocked and puzzled by my response.

"You didn't get the message out about when the show is airing, you didn't talk about this, and you didn't talk about that," I explained. "You didn't get your messages out. You need to play offense—so focus on those messages."

Since then she has knocked every interview out of the park.

There are three basic kinds of interviews that you'll be expected to do: print, radio, and TV. For all types, you'll want to know a couple of things before going into the interview. Always ask the interviewer how long the talk is expected to last and what the basis of the discussion will be. Then take down the reporter's number, collect your thoughts, and call back. Before you call back, pull up his or her previous clips on the Internet. If you've never heard of the reporter, find out whether he or she is a hatchet guy or a softball tosser. Again, the objective is to avoid surprise.

If it's a print interview, you'll have longer than a typical two-minute radio or TV interview. This allows you to get more of your anecdotes in and to repeat your messages. Keep in mind that what you don't say, they can't put in. So never be combative and never appear to be stonewalling. Remember that you've always got to appear accessible and charming, even while you're avoiding their tough questions like the plague.

If you're doing a radio interview or a print interview by phone, go in a room where it's quiet, and have a piece of paper in front of you listing your messages and your anecdotes. Don't multitask while you're doing the interview—it's not a good time for checking your e-mail or the length of your toenails. Just because no one is watching doesn't mean no one's noticing whether you're dialed in or not. If *you* don't find yourself compelling to listen to, why should anyone else? Focus on the questions, get out your messages, and use your anecdotes, and, where necessary, bridge back to what you want to say.

I need to say something here about writing things down. Except when I am in a swimming pool, I virtually always have a pad and pen with me. (I'm not as high-tech as the younger generation, who text themselves.) At my first PR job, on the first day, everyone at the company told me the legendary story of an account executive who showed up at a meeting without paper or a writing instrument. He was fired immediately after the meeting. I learned two things: one, to bring pen and paper, and two, don't trust your memory. If it's important to remember, write it down.

If you're going to do a group on-camera interview where there will be two or three guests talking, claim your territory with the other guests before the interview begins. If the subject is the environment, you might tell another guest, "You talk about the health effects of environmental hazards, and I'll talk about what people can do." It's like a basketball team—you can't take all the shots, and you've all got different strengths or weaknesses. You might be better up close to the basket, in the paint, while the other guest might be better from the three-point line. When you take the initiative and establish who will handle which type of question, you make for a smoother group interview, and you also establish your dominance over the others.

Now that you know what to say, let's talk about what you shouldn't say during an interview. First, never trust reporters. They are not your friends—they have a job to do. There's no such thing anymore as "off the record." Anything you tell a reporter at any time is fair game and may come back to bite you.

Second, when you're preparing for a TV show, people will be coming in and miking you. Don't ever assume anything is private from the time you step into the building, and especially once you get that microphone on. Basically, if you've got something to say that you don't want the whole world to hear, keep your mouth shut until you get back in your car.

Third, if you're doing a talk show, assume that anything you say during commercial breaks can be picked up by the audience. For example, when I do *Larry King Live* or any other show on CNN, I know that the commercials may only appear to the American audience. The rest of the world can see me and the other guests sitting in our chairs and chatting—and they can hear every word. Be careful and don't say something you wouldn't want the whole world to hear. This brings to mind the infamous moment when Ronald Reagan went live on what he thought was a dead microphone and announced signing "legislation that will outlaw Russia forever. We begin bombing in five minutes." He got in trouble for that, but it might have increased the Soviets' fear or even paranoia about him, so maybe it wasn't such a bad thing. But you're not Ronald Reagan, so don't take the chance. In short, never say anything you don't want in the press.

Fourth, don't speculate. Reporters often like to ask questions that call for speculative answers, like "Senator, if it turns out that the price of oil climbs another twenty dollars, a million Americans could be thrown out of work. What would you do in that situation?" The best answer is along these lines: "Well, I'm not a mind reader. I don't speculate." Then take your bridge back to your messages—that's what a well-media-trained interviewee does: "But the high price of oil is a reminder to all of us that we have to continue to develop alternative sources of energy if our country is going to be energy sufficient by the year 2050, which is one of my goals." Nice move, huh?

Fifth, don't use the term "No comment." We see people saying that on TV all the time. In the eyes of the viewer, it's the same as saying, "Yes, I did it," or, worse, "Screw you." Instead, you can avoid commenting on things in a somewhat more courteous manner, one which will put you in a better light—as in, "I'm not going to comment on that, because it's too personal." Or, "I'm not going to comment on that, because it's in litigation." Or, "I'm not going to comment on that, because I'm not aware of the situation." The common thread here: always tell them why you're not going to comment, and then keep your mouth shut. Home run slugger Mark McGwire lost the admiration of baseball fans in a heartbeat when he repeatedly told Congress, "I'm not here to talk about the past." Then why are we here?

Sixth, what happens if you get a phone call a few days after the interview asking for more information? Those calls typically begin with a transparent ruse such as "My editor wants a little more clarification on the story." What they're really saying is, "You were too much on message, and I need some help getting a more controversial story." Since I represent major celebrities, my antennae go up when I get those phone calls. I'm very polite, but I always tell them, "I'm sorry, but my client doesn't do more than one interview." I invite them to e-mail questions because my client is very busy. If the questions turn out to be factual matters—when they were born, what high school they attended, when they killed their first wife—I'll answer. If it's about providing a clarification, no problem. But if it's about opening up new lines of questioning, my lips are sealed.

Seventh, if your interviewer gets your name or another salient fact wrong, correct him simply and politely. If *you* make a misstatement, correct yourself and go on; don't call attention to it. There's no reason to let an error go unchecked. It doesn't mean that you should go off on the interviewer or walk off the set. A simple correction will get it done.

Finally, know your areas of expertise. Know what you know, but more important, know what you don't know. Don't get into those death spirals that begin with the words "I'm not a lawyer but . . ." or "I'm not a doctor but . . ." or "I never played in the NFL but . . ." If you don't know, it's okay to say so. Instead, use your bridge to get back to a message, as in, "I'm not a doctor, but as someone who's suffered from the disease, I can tell you . . ." Got it?

Remember that almost every media interview you do may end up on the Internet, so be careful about what you say. You don't want to come across as glib or dishonest, because that interview will be hanging out in cyberspace for the next two million years. It's just not worth the hassle.

Humor can be a good tool in interviews, with some caveats. Number one: what are you talking about? If it's a heavy topic like illness or war, humor won't work well. Number two: keep it clean. Number three: you have to be comfortable using humor. If you aren't funny, even having the best joke writer in the business won't help you. In that case, don't be afraid to smile. A smile is always a good thing.

One of my British friends recently used a term I love: the barbecue factor. It translates to this question: "Would I like to have a barbecue in my backyard with that guy?" Do you have the barbecue factor?

Let's also talk about dressing for success. What do you wear on any given show? The best way to determine the answer is to watch the show repeatedly. Record it for a few days and note the decor and the clothing of other guests. *Oprah*'s set features cream-colored sofas. So a cream-colored skirt won't do. Another show might have a red background, so you certainly don't want to wear red. In the famous 1960 Nixon-Kennedy presidential debates, JFK wore a blue suit and Vice President Nixon wore a gray suit. Even though the debate was presented in black and white, Kennedy's blue suit "popped" more against the gray background, and it made him look, as we say today, more presidential.

Whatever you wear, avoid fabrics with checks and a lot of pattern because they will create a moiré effect, which means that your outfit will turn into an electric blur. Also, dress authentically. Some people have uniforms—you always know who they are by what they wear. Al Davis, owner of the Oakland Raiders, always wears silver and black. Richard Simmons pretty much always wears the same type of gym clothes. Bruce Vilanch on *Hollywood Squares* wore his famous T-shirts and red glasses. Matt Drudge never appears in public without his 1940s newsman-style fedora. Older readers will recall Minnie Pearl, who would wear clothing with the thrift shop tags still on them when she appeared on the *Grand Ole Opry*. The most dangerous show for celebrity women, surprisingly, is *Regis and Kelly*. With those high stools, if a woman guest wears a skirt that's too short, it's good morning, America.

Dressing authentically can make a big difference in terms of your career. In 1976, Jimmy Carter scored major points with the electorate when he was shown carrying his own suit bag to a presidential debate in Philadelphia. Whatever you wear, don't be too wild. It's not a fashion show, and you don't want your clothing to distract from your message.

Perhaps the exception that proves the rule is when Pamela Anderson went on *The Tonight Show* wearing a white afro three feet in diameter. Jay Leno was dumbstruck. However, just because it works for Pamela Anderson doesn't mean it will work for the rest of us. Don't let your clothing say more than you do. Women should look well-tailored and men should favor suits and sports coats. Keep it simple.

A word about hair: women, make sure your haircut is appropriate, flattering, and easy to maintain. Don't change your hair every three weeks, because it can become news. Every time Katie Couric does something new with her hair, someone somewhere feels compelled to write about it. Try to stick to a color palette one finds in nature. And whether it's clothing or hair, age-appropriateness is hugely important.

For men, a bad toupee or a comb-over just won't cut it anymore. When you wear an obvious toupee, the message you're sending is that you're not comfortable with who you are. You look like you have something to hide. (You do—your bald head.) And even Rudy Giuliani got rid of his bad comb-over.

In terms of fragrances, less is more. Until they invent Smell-avision, what's the point? Some people are allergic to fragrances, and some fragrances are just plain repellant.

Most people have video cameras, so test your look well in advance of heading to the studio. Before you go on TV, make sure you look in the mirror. How do you look? Fabulous, no doubt. But just the same, comb your hair, powder your face, wipe the sweat off, get that little piece of spinach out from between your teeth. Since you're going to be on TV, where people judge you not just for what you say but for how you look when you're saying it, be a little more animated and energetic than usual. That couple of minutes that they tape will boil down to a ten-second sound bite—if you're lucky. So be "on"—without going over the top—at all times.

Now let's talk about posture once you're on the set. Don't lean back in the chair. Instead, put your butt all the way back, and men, sit on the back of your sport coat, or it will lump up behind you. Men and women ought to lean forward as they sit, because that grants them a more powerful persona. It means your head is a little closer to the camera and it means that it's easier to bring your hands up toward your face in order to gesture. You want to have an almost athletic look, as if you are ready to pounce. If you're leaning back it's tough to pull that off. In fact, the only one who could lean back in a chair and still do a credible interview was William F. Buckley Jr., and he's dead, so don't try it. I don't care how big and cushy the chair is. You're not there to rest. You're there to get your messages out.

One of the worst messaging experiences I ever had was with O. J. Simpson when he was doing commercial endorsements following a stellar collegiate and professional football career. One of our clients was a huge financial firm, and they were having a golf tournament. They paid tens of thousands of dollars for Simpson to attend their event. We were in the car headed to a television talk show, and I was telling him the name of the sponsor and asking him to please mention it if he could, Of course, O. J. never mentioned the client on air. Arrogance is no substitute for paying attention.

Once you're in the chair, try not to bounce and wiggle and shimmy. A decade ago, I did a lot of media training for younger actors at Nickelodeon. One of the young people in the group was Amanda Bynes. Amanda, who has since gone on to a notable career as an actress, couldn't stop bouncing in her chair. She was young at the time and that behavior was more acceptable. Some kids just bounce. We toned her down a little bit, and today she gives a great interview.

You'll know in advance on which show you're going to appear, so check it out before you do your interview. Whether it's Anderson Cooper or Leno or Oprah, or a local show, watch it for a few days. How did the interviewer conduct the interviews? What does he/she wear? How does he/she ask questions? Who do you like and who don't you like? It sounds so simple, but so many people don't do it, always to their detriment. Again, surprise is the enemy.

Don't drink a lot of caffeine before an interview. You don't want to look too wired on TV. If I can get slightly scientific for a moment, when you know you have to do an interview, you get excited and your body produces epinephrine. Once that stuff starts kicking in, you get jumpy. So half an hour before the show, run around the block, do some jumping jacks, just move.

After the epinephrine has done it's work, norepinephrine kicks in, which will mellow you out, make you calmer, and allow you to focus better. Also, don't drink anything really hot or really cold before the show. Herbal tea is best, or water at room temperature. Ice water closes up your throat. You don't want that, do you? Of course not.

What if you have followed all my suggestions, thoughtfully prepared and practiced, but are still apprehensive about interviewing? You look great, feel good, and you know not to be surprised if the interviewer digs up some dirt, but you are still afraid that they will catch you off guard. Here's a technique I used with Dr. Bernard Lewinsky, Monica's dad, whose family had been beaten up badly by the media and who was looking to defend his daughter and protect his family's image. I had him write out the ten worst questions he could be asked on the air. Do this for yourself. Know the answers for the ten worst possible questions someone could ask you.

Once you can answer those questions, nothing else will frighten you. If you're prepared for them, you'll be able to answer anything. Once you've done that, write another list of questions, both good and bad. Practice answering them using a video recorder, and have the interviewer be played by a coworker, a friend, your spouse or partner—just so long as it's someone who will give you objective advice. The more you practice, the more confident you'll be. Good luck.

So that's Howard's Media Training 101 course. Be smart, be sassy, be authentic, be funny but not glib, but above all . . . stick to your messages. Bridge back when you have to. Have your anecdotes ready. And knock it out of the park.

CHAPTER 10

ALL SYSTEMS GO: THE PRELAUNCH CHECKLIST

Before it launches the space shuttle into orbit, NASA always takes it through a prelaunch sequence to make sure that all systems are, as they say at Cape Canaveral, a "go." If you're reading this book on a jet, the pilot took the aircraft through a prelaunch checklist for the same reason. And when you're about to launch your PR campaign, it makes sense for you to do the same thing. Before you pull the trigger, make sure you're ready.

The last thing you want to do is launch a public relations campaign without ensuring that your Web site is current and that all the links operate properly, your letterhead, business cards, and Web site are all of the same basic design, your messages are clear and coherent, and you have a critical mass of distribution for your product. Why create demand if consumers can't buy it? This, by the way, is one of the most consistent mistakes eager entrepreneurs make. This is the time to look over everything we've done so far in this book and make sure that you have checked each box to your utmost satisfaction. Let's take a look at exactly what needs to be reviewed before you are ready to launch:

1. Have you done appropriate research on yourself, both on the Internet and in print sources? Have you performed the "opposition research" that a political campaign would perform, not just on the other candidate but on its own candidate, so that you are aware of the positives and the negatives that may be out there? Have you taken the pulse of the community into which you intend your messages to be projected? Do you know how people feel about you right now?

2. Have you created your three to five messages, and do they match up with the who, what, where, when, and why—basic questions of journalism? If somebody woke you at two in the morning, would you be able to recite those messages perfectly, with the clarity of a serviceman stating his name, rank, and serial number? Are you clear about what you want to tell the world? And why?

3. Have you done your media prep? Do you have your anecdotes ready to go along with your messages? Could you do a five-minute interview, and could you spin out enough material to talk for an hour? Can you bridge back from questions you don't like to the messages you want to present? Can you answer your "ten worst questions"?

4. Is all of your material in order? Is your Web site up? Have you tested the links? Can you buy your product and find your own e-mail address and phone number? Again, is the look and feel of all of your materials, from your business cards to your letterhead, all of a piece? Do you have the right number of photos and videos up on your Web site? (The "right number" means just enough so that people can get a sense of who you are and what you stand for, but not so many that they'll think you're a raving egotist for having so many images of yourself up on your site.)

5. Have you created your media matrix, showing all of the various audiences that you can address with your messages—and have you sussed out all of the different newspapers, magazines, Web sites, bloggers, persons of influence, and so on where your messages could appear?

6. *I think of this process as similar to what you see on the design shows*, where they pull together color chips, furniture samples, perhaps a little piece of carpet, maybe a vase standing over there, and then they ask themselves, "Does this all work together? Have I formed a cohesive whole?" If something doesn't look right, this is the time to take it out. And even if it all looks great to you, this is the time to have someone else take a look at the whole package for you. If you haven't had a second pair of eyes reviewing everything you have created in order to get out your messages, do it now.

If you've achieved all that you need to create your campaign, the next question is, How do you get the word out? Messages can spread virally, as they did in the case of John Amaechi, who became the first NBA player to come out as a gay man. In this instance, local stories led to national stories, and those led to international stories. How do you go about that? Perhaps a news conference is the better way to go, or a press release, to announce something of a timely nature. When Kristine Lefebvre went on the cover of *Playboy*, you can be sure we got the word out in a hurry.

The next question to ask is how to vary the story slightly so that different media outlets get seemingly different stories. You don't want everybody to be running the same thing. If there's a tech angle, then you want to be increasing the importance of the tech side of the story for *Wired* or the tech section of the newspaper. If there's a business aspect to your story, that's what you want to play up for the major business publications.

Often people ask me about the idea of doing exclusives (only one placement per industry or media outlet), and my response is that this is something that only professionals should attempt. We might provide a print exclusive to one newspaper, a broadcast exclusive to one network, a business exclusive to a major business publication, and so on. We do so because we might want to work a little more closely with one journalist, which would be an attempt to control the content of the story more thoroughly. This is one of the few cases where it would not be appropriate for an individual to attempt what PR professionals do every day. It can be like playing with dynamite. By giving a story to one person, you might alienate someone else, and that person may never want to cover you again. It's just not worth it unless you know exactly what you're doing.

How do you offer a different story to multiple outlets, on either an exclusive or nonexclusive basis? Let's say that a company is launching a new detergent. The Business section won't be interested in the fact that it protects delicate fabrics. That would be a good story for a Home or Style section. On the other hand, the Business section of your local newspaper would be very interested in the fact that your company believes it will increase market share because the new product is environmentally friendly. See what I mean?

It's also worth asking, before you pitch a story to a newspaper, TV, or radio station, if that outlet usually covers those types of stories. See where you'll fit in. Would a story like this typically receive a paragraph, or would it get a whole story? The same story might be big news in a small town but only rate minor mention in a larger locale. Keep your expectations in line with reality—be realistic about what kind of coverage you'll get.

You've done all your homework, and now it's time to launch. How do you know that the time is right for your messages to get out to the world? That's the subject of the next chapter.

CHAPTER 11

PULLING THE TRIGGER: THE PUBLICIZABLE MOMENT

The publicizable moment is the moment that pulls the trigger on everything you've done so far to create your campaign. Here are some examples of typical publicizable moments:

- ➤ A news release going out
- ➤ The filing of a lawsuit
- ➤ A court decision
- ➤ An event
- ➤ A press junket for a movie
- ➤ An advertising campaign launch
- ➤ Announcing that you're running for office in your community
- ➤ Announcing that you're forming a group to clean up a river
- ➤ Opening a business
- ➤ A satellite media tour or a standard media tour
- ➤ An election
- ➤ A speech
- ➤ A convention

➤ A research report, or white paper

➤ Or, in my business, releasing to TMZ.com a gossip item that you control

Understand that *you control* when the media is going to cover you—it's your decision, because you choose your launch date. You choose the publicizable moment that launches your campaign. So, what makes the most sense for you?

If you are in retail, the Friday after Thanksgiving is a perfect time for the creation of a publicizable moment. That day is called Black Friday, not because bad things happen on that day, but because retailers typically go into the black on the Friday after Thanksgiving after essentially having broken even during the prior eleven months of the year. When I worked with Spiegel, we created events to show off the hottest gifts for the Christmas season. When I worked with the high-end Century City shopping center in West Los Angeles, the Friday after Thanksgiving was a great day for drawing publicity to the stores there.

Another former client of mine who takes advantage of this special day is ComScore.com. ComScore is able to draw attention to itself on the Friday after Thanksgiving and on the Monday after— now known as CyberMonday—by letting the world know what to look for in the stores this season, who's shopping where, what the hot shopping Web sites are, and how shopping over the Internet compares with brick and mortar stores. You always want to ask yourself how you can tie your messages to events on the calendar, or events that you create for yourself.

In the business world, publicizable moments are often of the financial variety. When a company announces its earnings or has a "material" announcement—one likely to influence the company's share price—that's definitely a moment to seize from a public relations standpoint. The timing is often dictated by the Securities and Exchange Commission.

Now it's time to choose the best setting or backdrop for your publicizable moment. Think about presidential campaigns, because a lot of time and effort goes into choosing the right backdrop for political events. Typically, candidates announce their candidacies in front of schools, ecological sites to which they wish to call attention, or anyplace where Mom, apple pie, and happy voters can be found. Intriguingly, when Mitt Romney announced his failed presidential candidacy in 2007, he didn't choose his adoptive state of Massachusetts, where he was the governor. Instead, he went to Michigan to announce, because Michigan is a swing state laden with electoral votes. The media was given the story that he was going back to his heritage, the state where his father was a popular governor—but you and I know the truth. It was all about those electoral votes. He didn't have a chance in Massachusetts, yet he won the Michigan primary.

By contrast, some politicians really mess up their publicizable moments. Senator Fred Thompson waited too long to announce his 2008 candidacy. By the time he finally did, people rolled their eyes and said, "What else is new?" He failed to benefit as much as he could have from a guaranteed publicizable moment because his timing was so far off. He also tried to copy another actor by announcing his candicacy on Jay Leno's show. He ended up showing that he wasn't as good as the first to do it, and it felt "me too" and unoriginal.

Someone who really got it right was Arnold Schwarzenegger, the governor of California, who was the first to announce his candidacy on *The Tonight Show*. This was a smart move because Arnold has a natural affinity with entertainment audiences, and because Leno is an old friend of Arnold's creating a comfortable environment. The bottom line: choose your publicizable moment wisely, and let it be authentic to who you are, what you stand for, and what you are trying to accomplish. There's a big difference between announcing a marriage in the *National Enquirer* and doing it with an elegant black-and-white picture in the *New York Times*. Make the right choice.

Sometimes a publicizable moment is thrust upon you, and it's up to you to recognize that it's there . . . and to grab it. Remember Clara Peller, the dear old lady of the "Where's the beef?"

ads that were extremely successful for the Wendy's hamburger chain? Those commercials were languishing in relative obscurity until a seniors' group protested the use of a "little old lady" in an ad. All of a sudden, the attention of the nation was focused on those ads—and Wendy's ran with it, brilliantly so. My message here: if a publicizable moment comes along, grab it.

Sometimes you can create one out of whole cloth. One of the most important classes I took in college was statistics, because I learned how to parse numbers in so many different ways. In the movie industry, where I do a lot of my work, playing with statistics is an art form. Ever heard of a movie described as "the largest nonholiday animated opening ever"? Huh? It just shows that somebody with a good grasp of statistics found a great way to make a movie look more important than it was. There's nothing wrong with that—they aren't lying, and it's just show biz. In the business world, of course, numbers matter. And sometimes what number your company is can make a huge difference in its perception in the marketplace. When I was working with L.A. Gear, the company discovered that it was the third largest sneaker company after Nike and Reebok. I pointed out that this was a highly publicizable fact. We generated a *Los Angeles Times* story to show the business media that we ought to be mentioned in the same breath with Nike and Reebok, and emphasized the big gap between us and the shoe manufacturers who were four, five, and six on the list.

Similarly, Hollywood used to speak of the "big three" talent agencies, an expression that sat well everywhere except with executives of the fourth largest talent agency, UTA, which happened to be a client of ours at the time. UTA represented major stars like Jim Carrey at the peak of his career and was a rising talent agency. We wanted to change the perception of Hollywood from the "big three" to the "big four." So whenever a journalist did a story talking about the big three, we would make a phone call and explain that the "big three" wasn't 100 percent accurate. Contrary to what you may have heard, journalists love accuracy—they can't argue with the facts. Before long, the media, and then Hollywood itself, was referring to the "big four" talent agencies, our client among them. You always want to be on the lookout for how to reposition yourself with the use of statistics that favor your cause.

The next technique I want to share with you is the creation of what I call the noncontroversial controversy. At one point we represented the city of Fort Worth, Texas, which is quite a cosmopolitan place. The Bass and Hunt families call Fort Worth home, as do Radio Shack, Pier One Imports, and many other leading companies. For a small town, Fort Worth has great culture—three world-class art museums and the Van Cliburn piano competition. Yet Fort Worth was known, especially in its rival city, Dallas, as Cow Town, and it wanted to change its image.

City executives turned not to a Dallas agency, of course, but to the Chicago branch of an international agency where I then worked. We created a PR campaign to improve the image of Fort Worth in the eyes of the media and Texans generally. While this campaign was going on, I opened an issue of *Crain's Chicago Business*, a local business publication, and found a two-page ad paid for by the Illinois Department of Commerce and Community Affairs, making fun of Texas. The idea behind the ad was that Illinois had it all over Texas as a place to do business. The ad made fun of typical Texas stereotypes and accents. This was a great opportunity for a noncontroversial controversy.

I called the editor of *Crain's Chicago Business* and offered him an opinion column written by the head of the Fort Worth corporation about how Texas had Illinois beat. They loved the idea—the media loves controversy—and the article was written and appeared in *Crain's* along with a photo of DFW Airport, which was new at the time. Illinois paid a ton of money for their ad; we paid nothing and got even more publicity than they did.

But it didn't stop there. Once the opinion column from the head of the Fort Worth corporation ran, we started calling the press. "Hey, there's a war going on between Illinois and Texas." The story went everywhere and even appeared in the *New York*

Times and moved on the AP wire. Everyone won—both Texas and Illinois—because the story brought business opportunities in both locations to the eyes of the general business community. That's what I mean by a noncontroversial controversy.

If you want a more recent one, think about the on-air "spats" between Donald Trump and Rosie O'Donnell. Were they really mad at each other? Of course not. They were both delighted to have an opportunity to be in the media spotlight—a place that neither of them finds easy to resist.

Sometimes going into the lion's den can be a publicizable moment. Bill Clinton criticized political activist Sister Souljah to great effect, reinforcing his position against extremism. It is now known as a "Sister Souljah Moment."

Now let's discuss "opportunistic PR"—when a moment occurs related to a subject on which you're the expert, and you find a way to leverage yourself into the story. As an example, a story came out about the taxes that celebrities must pay on the expensive gifts they receive at red carpet events. One of our clients, GBK Productions, creates elegant gifting suites, where celebrities get free things. Instead of shying away from the story, we jumped into the fray by talking about the tax advantages of gifting suites versus gift bags. During the 2008 writers' strike, when the Golden Globe awards were canceled, the charismatic owner of the company, Gavin Keilly, got media coverage by talking about how the strike was hurting the "little guy." We got over the criticism of celebrities—many of whom are already wealthy—receiving expensive free things by promoting the "giving suites," where charities could get donations, celebrity participation, and attention, and enlist the help of stars.

Research is also an important launch point for publicity. Qualitative research—points of view, theories—can be released in white papers, to much media acclaim. Quantitative research—i.e., numbers—is a huge part of the media's diet. If you can quantify something, you're halfway home. Here are three examples of quantitative research. My company once represented EDI. It's a boring-sounding name, but they tell you who won the box office every weekend. We're the people who made the "top five box office" derby a Monday morning staple of pop culture, in order to get our client's name out there. Also, early in my career, I represented a company that did events for college students on spring break. The detailed research they conducted on site got them stories and made them experts on the young adult marketplace throughout the year. And finally, Moët & Chandon does an annual "Moët Index" of pricing for luxury goods—always including caviar and, of course, Moët & Chandon champagne.

This whole business of publicizable moments—of public relations in general—is part art and part science. There's never going to be an answer that works 100 percent of the time. It's the same concept with prescription drugs—you could give a hundred people a medication and ninety-nine will see their problem go away while one will break out in hives or experience some other undesirable side effect. Your messages can be affected by whatever else happens in the news that day, the mood of the reporter, even the weather. Who knows? Public relations is not 100 percent controllable, but that's why you're sending your story to many different outlets. Surely most of them will get your story right.

The last thought about the publicizable moment I want to share with you is this question: is the moment authentic and credible, and will it achieve what you intend? To illustrate this point, I want to take you back to the Monica Lewinsky episode in American culture. Her attorney did a piece about a legal aspect of the case for the *Los Angeles Daily Journal,* our local daily law newspaper. I asked the attorney what he wanted to have happen with the story once it appeared in *Daily Journal.* "What do you mean?" he asked me. "How do you expect the story to get out there?" I asked. He told me, "It'll just get out there." And I told him, "It doesn't really work like that. Stories don't just get out there—you have to help them."

In other words, just because you have created a publicizable moment, and you have published a story somewhere, it doesn't mean that the media will suddenly flock to your door. A story might exist in the minds of the media for a day or so, but then it could die, as did Monica Lewinsky's attorney, in this case. The story lay there and had no "legs," as we call it in the business. Once you've had your publicizable moment, how do you keep your story alive? How do you give your messages "legs"? That's the subject of the next chapter.

CHAPTER 12

KEEP ON TRUCKIN': HOW TO MAKE MOMENTUM WORK FOR YOU

A public relations campaign is a marathon, not a sprint. You're in it for the long haul. The announcement of your publicizable moment launches your campaign, but as the song says, "We've only just begun." In this chapter, I'd like to talk about how PR professionals help stories grow legs—so that you can keep your messages in the public eye for an extended period of time.

Think back to the 1992 Democratic Presidential Convention, when Bill Clinton chose Al Gore as his running mate. Typically, presidential campaigns went on hiatus from the time of the political conventions until Labor Day. But Clinton wisely took advantage of the momentum the Gore nomination and the entire Democratic convention created. He and Gore embarked on a multistate "bus tour," touring the nation like rock stars, keeping the electricity and their newsworthiness alive. You've experienced your publicizable moment, but what's your "bus tour" going to be like? The launch shouldn't be the only arrow in your quiver. What are you going to do to keep your story fresh? The challenge is frequency. How do you keep your story in the public eye multiple times?

The first thing to do is to plan different moments that will also be publicizable over the course of the campaign. Let's say that you're running for city council. As you hit certain fund-raising goals or get key endorsements, you're making news. Have your list ready, so that when you reach those events, you'll have a system in place to get the story out. Either you, a team member, or someone you bring onboard will write the press release. If there's an approval process, that should happen quickly, and within a few keystrokes, it's out to your list. Political campaigns, most ongoing businesses, and just about anything that's interesting to the public generates news on a sporadic or regular basis. Every time you make news, make sure that everybody knows about it.

We discussed a list of "publicizable moments" in the previous chapter. These same moments can be used to keep momentum going in a campaign.

Having a system in place to get the story out quickly is vital. Reinventing the wheel every time is not a good idea. If that happens, then you might have missed something in the prelaunch phase, most likely in establishing your media matrix and your contact list. You can also go too far with this kind of thing; there's a PR person in New York who somehow got me on his list, and I now think of him as the spammer from hell, because every time he signs a client, I get an e-mail from him. Similarly, there's a particular city council member (whose name I won't mention) from whom it seems I get a press release announcing every time he goes to the men's room. You really can overdo it. It's the "boy who cried wolf" syndrome. So be realistic about what is newsworthy, what you should announce, and what you should not. If you're running for city council in Cedar Rapids, Iowa, it will be easier to make news under those circumstances than if you're running for city council in Manhattan. Every time you send out news, you may not get a big article or TV story right away. But you're building a cadre, if you will, of journalists who are aware of your campaign. When you show that you are creating regular news, you're demonstrating momentum. Reporters take note of that. They'll say, "Wow, that person has raised a lot of money, gotten big endorsements, proposed intriguing programs, is offering interesting options to customers," or whatever the case may be. That will prompt them, more often than not, to take a second look at you. Your job is to strike a balance between being a pest and being informative.

When you send the news out, don't just send it to the media. That same announcement should go out to your staff, other internal audiences, financial backers, neighborhood groups—your entire e-mail list. As we discussed earlier, your multiple publics are broader than just the media. Be sure to keep everyone in the loop about what you are doing. Again, people who are close to you, either because they are backing you financially, are employed by you, or are otherwise in an important and close relationship with you, be it business or personal, want to hear things from you before they see them on the front page of the newspaper.

Another way to give a story "legs" is to create trend stories. Let's say you own a dry cleaning establishment with a unique, environmentally safe way to clean clothes. You might find that the paper is doing a story on businesses going green. Way before that happens, you should have taken the time to define who you are and what makes you unique among your competitors. By claiming your space and establishing a relationship with a small business writer in your locale, you'll be at the top of his or her mind when it comes to that story about green businesses. You want more than just the small business writer to know about what you're doing. For example, the fashion writer might be interested in a story about the worst stain possible on an expensive piece of clothing and how you can take it out in an environmentally sensitive manner. Or maybe you're an immigrant who managed to get away from harsh conditions in your country of origin; now that you're in America, you've got that environmentally safe dry cleaning business, and your life story itself is newsworthy. So the person who does profiles, either for the general news section or the business news section of your local paper, ought to know about you. The environmental reporter ought to know about you, since you are so environmentally friendly. Read your local paper on a regular basis to see who's covering the "beats" that affect you. Take time to send them materials with special emphasis on the types of stories they cover. That way, when they read it, they'll make the connection—"Oh, I see. There's something going on environmentally here. I need to investigate this further." And that puts you back in the paper.

Here's another way to build a career: punditry. A pundit is someone who comments on things. We call ourselves "the green room club": people who do regular punditry on television shows. How do you get in the club? Get yourself a DVR and practice creating and speaking pithy remarks. To become a nationally recognized pundit, you don't necessarily have to leave your hometown. The thing to do is to get really big in your local market by offering yourself to the local stations as a wise and witty commentator on all things local and perhaps national as well. That way, if something worthy of national news attention happens in your locale, the network will turn to you. If something big and newsworthy happens in your community, turn to your contacts at the local station and say, "Tell the network about me." In those situations, networks are always looking for someone local and smart who can help them.

Compile your own clip reel. Aggregate your TV appearances on YouTube.com. Send the link to clients, potential clients, and anyone you can think of who can further your broadcasting career. Market your best lines. Don't just say them—make them work for you again and again.

If you're going to work the talk show circuit, you must have some compelling issue. Maybe you've created something—an environmental program that's replicable in communities across the nation. Showcase it by finding other complementary businesses, as we discussed earlier, and present the lot of you as a package to the producers of appropriate shows. Producers are always at their wits' end trying to figure out something new to do. Never hesitate to suggest an episode to the producers of *Tyra, Dr. Phil*, or whatever show makes the most sense for you.

Perhaps you have an unusual or quirky skill. Many shows, including *Ellen DeGeneres* and *The Tonight Show with Jay Leno*, like quirky people who can do quirky things. As I like to say, be outrageous, because it's the only place that isn't crowded. Put your unusual talent on Facebook.com and market it. Light the fuse and hope it goes viral. E-mail the link to everyone you know. Send it to blogs and Web sites. Put your video on your page. If you remember back to the 2004 presidential election, the individuals who were creating animations of Bush and Kerry during that campaign on JibJab.com were able to turn it into a lucrative business.

Sometimes you just feel like you're out of ideas. It happens to all of us. Or, maybe the ideas you're pitching just aren't working. When we get into that situation, we often have a "brainstorming session." There are a lot of names for these meetings but they are all creative ideation sessions where people get together to develop ideas. I'm going to tell you how to do them simply and effectively.

The first thing you need to know is what you're looking for going in. Are you looking for ideas for stories to pitch to the media? Are you looking for potential sponsors? Are you looking for ways to make your brand or company more exciting or ways to develop a brand extension? The more specific you are with what you need going in, the more successful your ideation session will be.

The first thing to do is to select three to seven people to take part in the session for a specific period of time. Any more than seven people and the session will likely be confusing; more than an hour or two and your participants will get burned out.

Before a session, I like to send out a briefing document so the participants' brains can start working ahead of time. This document tells what the goals of the session are and gives detailed information on the product or business that they will be thinking about. If possible, send a sample ahead of time. I often ask the participants to write down five ideas before the session. These can be used when there is a lull in the session or as thought starters.

When your participants gather, have them do it in a place where you won't be bothered. No telephones, no BlackBerries, and no interruptions to the flow of ideas. That just breaks the rhythm.

Make sure you set the table—either a conference table or a dining room table—with product ads, press releases, brochures, anything tangible and inspirational. Have pads of paper and plenty of writing instruments for each person. Colored pencils and graph paper can actually be good because some people think better when they write, draw, scribble, or doodle. Let them. It helps their ideation process.

One of the attendees serves as the facilitator. That person must have high energy and hopefully at least a little experience with facilitating groups. Either the facilitator or a second person can be the secretary for the group and take notes on every idea. While this can be done on a legal pad or a laptop, I prefer to use big easels, big paper, and marking pens. This way the group can be inspired by the volume of ideas they are turning out and you can organize like ideas together. Either pin them or tape them to the wall. Post-it makes large pads that are perfect for this purpose.

There are some simple rules of brainstorming. First, we're going for quantity—not quality. It's the job of the leader to pick the best ideas after the session—not in the middle of it.

Second, no negatives are allowed. People's ideas are like babies, and if you kill them they will not share another one with you. If someone says something stupid, and they will, challenge them to come up with another way to make it work without telling them that it was a stupid idea or that it just doesn't work. Be empowering.

Third and finally, build on other people's ideas. The whole point of the session is to create synergies with the belief that multiple people can come up with more and better ideas than any single person can.

Then go to town. Challenge them. Get the "talkers" in the group to start it moving or, if you're the facilitator, have a few ideas of your own.

If you've done it right, and long enough, you will have pages of notes after an hour. Type them up and then begin to organize them into different areas—story ideas, product extensions, program objectives. Then take these organized thoughts and begin to measure them against your initial objectives. With proper preparation and analysis, I promise a productive session and lots of good ideas.

Another technique I absolutely love is called the "backgrounder." If you call up a journalist and say, "Will you do a story on this topic?" they'll typically come up with a hundred reasons why they can't. They're too busy. They don't really cover that. Their editor doesn't like that kind of story. You don't want a no, you want a yes. So how do you get a yes from a journalist?

My suggestion: take him or her out for a backgrounder—coffee, breakfast, or lunch, just you, the reporter, and perhaps your PR person or a staffer along for the ride. Here's how it works. If I were publicizing that dry cleaning business, I'd call up the appropriate reporter and say, "Hey, I'm working with this dry cleaner who's doing this really amazing thing to protect the environment. Let me come down to the paper, buy you a cup of coffee, and tell you about the business." Or, if I were running for city council in Cedar Rapids, I'd call the political reporter and say, "I know forty people are running for city council, but I have a unique perspective. I was born here, raised my kids here, served on the PTA—I'd like to take you to lunch and talk about why I'm entering the race at this time."

Journalists are a curious lot—but they're also very busy. If you can make their life easier by handing them information about an intriguing story or an intriguing angle, you're making their lives easier. And they'll love you for it. (P.S.—journalists love free food.)

When I ask for "backgrounder" meetings, I get them 80 to 90 percent of the time. You might have a lower success rate initially, but that's okay. Before long, you'll receive a lot more yes's than no's. Always use a gentle technique; we're not trying to force a story on someone. Make it difficult for a journalist to say,

"No, I won't listen to your ideas." That's tantamount to them saying, "I don't care, and I don't want to learn any more." That's not how journalists think. They're busy, busy people and you have to respect that, but they will take time to meet you, especially if you're buying. Don't call on deadline, which is five P.M. at most daily newspapers.

Once you're in the background meeting, don't make it a hard sell. You want to take a more chatty approach, while at the same time you're working very hard to get your messages out. That's the balance you want to strike. When it's over, don't leave saying, "Okay, now we do a story?" That's wrong. Instead, send a handwritten note or e-mail immediately afterward saying "Thank you for your time and interest today. I'm really glad you responded to my experience on the PTA and how it's going to translate into my serving the community on the city council." Always come from your vision about who you'll be when your goal is reached.

This is also a good time to send a link to your Web site: "Here's a link to the position paper I mentioned," or, "Here's a copy of the book that we talked about that really changed my life." A small gesture like that goes a really long way. If you're wondering whether that's "buying the media," it's not. If you can buy them with a twenty dollar book, that doesn't say much about their integrity. What you're trying to do is establish a human bond between you and a person who represents a very powerful institution that can have a lot of influence on what you want to accomplish in the world.

Let's say that your efforts lead to someone doing a story on you, and I know they will. Don't call the reporter and say something to the effect of, "Thank you for doing a story on me." That makes it seem as though the reporter is just one more cog in the public relations machine. Instead, say, "Thank you for listening to what I had to say and really getting it, and writing a very fine story," or, "Thank you for writing about this very important topic and giving me a chance to get my opinion out there." That's a heck of a lot better than "Thanks for doing a story on me."

Another way to keep yourself in the public eye is to package a story for the journalist. You've now had your publicizable moment, you've been sending out news releases about what's happened since, you've sat down with the key journalists in your world, and you've had backgrounders with the people who cover your field. As we've discussed, journalists are very busy. You can get back into the public eye by building and packaging a story for them. Let's go back to the example of the environmentally sensitive dry cleaner. You own that store, and you've got a friend across town with an environmentally sensitive car wash, and you know another business owner who has created a new model for recycling paper and glass. Instead of saying to the reporter, "How about doing another story on me?" you can say, "Obviously, environmentalism is all the rage. I've got three businesses here that would make a good feature."

You're probably wondering why you would want to get free publicity for the other two businesses. The simple answer is that if you don't, you may not get a story for your business alone. Since you're not getting the publicity for competing businesses, you are risking nothing. These are called "trends" stories, and in the media, the rule of thumb is that three is a trend.

Another example of this: I had an entertainment client whose mother was his manager. We all know about the "stage mother" syndrome, but she actually did a really good job for him. I found a couple of other stars who were also managed by their mothers, and I got a story in a major entertainment publication on mothers as professional managers. The point was to get my client in the magazine, and we were able to do so by positioning him as part of a trend.

You can also do a story against the trend. Even twenty-five years ago, people were talking about how high-tech the future would be. I had a client who made doors for trailer trucks. Pretty dull, huh? Hard to get in the newspaper. So we went against the grain. He was acquiring other low-tech businesses in the region, so we built a story about how everyone else was going high-tech, but here's a guy going low-tech. We were all over the news.

The big kahuna in giving a story legs, the grand slam, is a profile all about you. Unless there's some immediate news going on, these take time to nurture. These stories have the biggest reach but the least frequency. If your paper does one on you now, it may be years before they do another one. Make sure that a story like this happens at the right time; when your campaign reaches a critical mass, that's the time to seek a major profile story.

What do you do when you're quoted in a story? What do you do when the story is all about you? You've got to market it. People no longer read the newspaper the way they used to. Circulations are declining, people are migrating to the Internet for news, and it's quite likely that the most important people on your list may never even have opened that day's newspaper, let alone found the story about you. Market the story—send it to your mailing list with an e-mail link so that they can easily find it. Reprint the story and send hard copies to the most important people on your list. It's not about just getting the story—you have to tell the people in your world that you got the story. Earlier, we said that half the battle is doing the work and the other half is letting the media know about it. Well, once the media knows about it and publishes it, it's up to you to tell everybody that the media has picked up on you and your messages.

Keep in mind that anything you do that's noteworthy is an opportunity to keep your messages in the public eye. Let's say that you're still the dry cleaner we discussed earlier, and now you're going to speak to the Cedar Rapids Chamber of Commerce about your environmentally friendly business. Before the speech, get listings in the paper, in relevant blogs, wherever you have an opportunity to put your name out there. Do a press release before the event and send it out to your list. At the event, take some photos. If an important person shows up, service (media-speak for "provide") the photos to the appropriate media. And then do a press release after the event about what you discussed. The headline might be "Joe Smith says every business needs to go green." Or, "Joe Smith tells Chamber of Commerce going green is good business."

How else do you keep momentum alive? Giving back is huge. Charity, caring about the community, and donations need not always be expressed in terms of $20 million gifts and your name on the building. You can do something as simple as starting an organic garden at an elementary school. Or you might create a neighborhood environmental fair and show people how to be more environmentally conscious at home. Simple things don't have to be enormous or expensive to have a powerful impact. Anything small yet meaningful will make a huge difference.

You also want to be careful about how and where you're seen. When celebrities show up too often for events, their presence ends up having no meaning. Certainly there's a lot of log rolling in any field. Someone goes to your event, you go to hers. There's an unspoken quid pro quo in these matters. Just don't allow yourself to be perceived as someone who will appear anywhere. In Hollywood, we say that some stars will appear at the opening of a filing cabinet, or a wound. That's not how you want to be defined. There's one Academy Award–nominated actress, whose name I won't mention, who attends red carpet events like all the other celebrities, but if she feels she didn't get enough flashbulbs, she'll walk around the side and do the red carpet again. I think that's a little excessive, don't you?

Another way to give your messages legs is to provide samples. If your business is built around your grandma's brownie recipe, then every appropriate journalist within thirty miles ought to have a plate of brownies on his or her desk. It's one thing for a car manufacturer to tell the auto trade reporters that a new car is fantastic, but there's no substitute for having reporters drive those cars. Perhaps you're a jeweler, and you're not in a position to give away a $200,000 necklace. But you can certainly loan your finest jewelry for important local events. Allow a local society reporter to see what it's like to wear a $200,000 necklace. In Hollywood we do it all the time. Jewelers lend celebrities jewelry, hoping that they'll like it . . . and not want to take it off. They also hope the photographers capture the jewels in a photo (and caption) that appears later in *People*. Top Beverly Hills jeweler Martin Katz became recognized the world over for his elegant jewelry by his loans on the red carpet.

Another trick we use is to create brand ambassadors—people with a special affinity toward the product we are promoting. We have given Hollywood power types budgets to entertain with certain liquors and invited them to exclusive parties for insiders only.

Another thing to consider is broadening your category. It's certainly a Hollywood phenomenon—athletes want to be actors, actors want to be politicians, singers want to act, and so on. Everybody's looking to broaden his or her category. Before Marion Jones lost her Olympic luster by abusing performance enhancing drugs, she was on the cover of *Vogue* magazine. That's because we were branding her and positioning her as someone who can wear something other than spandex. We wanted people to see another side of her, not just the incredibly fast woman. We wanted people to get to know her as a beautiful woman in remarkable shape. That way, she would be her own brand, so she could get endorsements and sponsorships. During the Olympic Games, there are hundreds of stories about the top athletes. But whose messages are still getting out there three weeks later? It happens with brands too. Michelob's campaign, "Weekends were made for Michelob," was so successful that they actually had to run another campaign letting you know that you could drink it during the week too.

Another way to keep the momentum going is to write a book. There are wonderful books out there about how to write, produce, and promote your own book, and about how to write book proposals. Or you can connect with a speakers bureau, which matches speakers with organizations, conventions, and meetings who need to hear about topics appropriate to their interests. Have a blog. It's time to have some real estate on the Web that people will visit. You've really got to be there now, so if you have any technophobia, it's time to get over it.

Who's the queen of "legs"? Who's perhaps the most effective

celebrity at keeping her story alive in front of the media? For my money, it's Madonna. As she likes to say, "I'm not the best singer and I'm not the best dancer, but I sure know how to push people's buttons." Love her or hate her, Madonna is courageous, takes risks, stays relevant, and remains in the news. She's not just "coming out with another album"; all of the moments in her life are newsworthy, from having a child to adopting a child from another country. I'm not telling you to adopt children in order to get publicity. What I am saying is that you want to go beyond the bounds of the normal expectations about people in your career path. Whatever you do, do it with style, panache, and authenticity. Be outrageous while being yourself, and your story will be like the Energizer Bunny—it will keep going and going. . . .

CHAPTER 13

SHOW ME THE INK: THE SECRETS OF PRESS AND RESULTS

S^{o far,} we have seen two definitions for PR. The first is the classic definition—public relations, meaning the way that you, your business, your ideas, or your products and services relate to the public. The second is the more modern definition of PR, Perception and Reality. When we talk about perception and reality, we're asking these questions: What perception, if any, is there in the marketplace right now about you and what you have to offer? Does that perception match the reality? If your perception is greater than your reality, and you are in the hype zone, then your ideas, campaigns, or businesses will eventually fall back to earth. If your reality is greater than the perception, then you are an unsung hero, without the success you deserve, unable to deliver the service that you offer.

So PR means how you relate to the public and how you align perception about you with the reality of who you are and what you offer. In this chapter, I want to introduce you to a third definition of PR—Press and Results. The big knock on public relations is that it cannot be measured. That's totally untrue. PR can be measured simply and effectively in the short term, in the middle, and over the long term. PR is almost always measurable. Let's see exactly how to measure the campaign you have created.

This third definition of PR breaks down into two ideas. The first is how much press you are receiving. The word "press" here encompasses everything from newspaper and magazine articles, to blurbs on the Web, to any other means by which your story is getting out to the world without the use of paid advertising. Second, "results" means exactly what the word says: What kinds of results are you getting? Are your sales going up? Are you reaching into a newer and more lucrative client base? Are your poll numbers tracking higher? Are more people coming up to you and saying, "I've made up my mind and I'm going to vote for you?" By any measure that you choose, how do the results compare with the goals you set for your campaign?

Let's begin by debunking the myth that PR is not measurable.

PR brings things to the party that advertising simply cannot buy. Typically, a PR campaign is part of a comprehensive program that includes commissionable advertising (that is, ads for which an ad agency would take a commission), Internet advertising, direct marketing, sales forces, and so on.

Big PR agencies measure their campaigns in very sophisticated ways. They will track many different variables: Where did the article appear? What is the circulation of that newspaper, magazine, or Web site where the piece appeared? How many times was the client mentioned? Was there a photo? What was the balance between positive and negative in the piece? Some companies actually invest in research before and after a program to see if the campaign "moved the needle." As we've discussed, journalists have to zing in a little negativity even in a mostly positive piece in order to retain the image of balance. You can never get a 100 percent positive piece unless your father-in-law happens to own the publication. Since that doesn't happen too often, we happily settle for a piece that is *mostly* positive.

That's a smart way to measure how your PR campaign is going. A not-so-smart way to measure it is to think of PR in terms of "advertising equivalency." This approach asks, "If the article about our client were an ad, how much would we have to pay for it?" For example, a one-page ad in *Time* magazine costs roughly $100,000. But it's silly to say that a mostly positive one-page article in *Time* magazine is worth only $100,000. As we've discussed repeatedly, an article is much more valuable than an ad, because of the third-party endorsement (and therefore credibility) factor. So the last thing you want to do is measure the effectiveness of your public relations against the standard of how much it would have cost you to buy that same space. You can purchase the space, but you cannot purchase the credibility.

Similarly, people will say they have "millions of dollars" of PR. As much as I'd like to believe that you can't place a ceiling on the value of PR, the "millions of dollars" figure is usually a bit farfetched. What exactly does that mean? Who spends millions of dollars on anything, aside from Budweiser, Ford, or Procter & Gamble? As much as I am a believer in PR, there's got to be a line somewhere as to just how effective it can be.

Sometimes, much to my chagrin, media relations work is called "free advertising." I have two things to say to that. Number one: "It ain't free." Number two: "It ain't advertising." Perhaps PR should be called earned media—it's earned by your ability to be creative, to hit the zeitgeist, to influence a journalist. Admittedly, the term "earned media" doesn't sparkle in the night, but it's considerably more accurate than free advertising or the concept of advertising equivalency. If you can get stories about yourself in publications, on radio and TV shows, and on Web sites, then you're doing something right. The question becomes just how much have you accomplished? The best way to answer that question is to be clear about your goals from the outset.

Here's an example. When John Amaechi and I met to discuss the publication of his book *Man in the Middle*, I asked him what his goals were. John was remarkably precise: He wanted a *New York Times* best seller. He wanted to make enough money from the book to afford to live in the United States and his native England. And he wanted to develop a speaking career in the United States. Those were the goals, and we achieved all of them. We delivered. The client was happy and so were we.

Sometimes things are a bit more murky. I represented a health club in Chicago early in my career. I got it a lot of attention, but the family that owned the business never seemed to be happy. So I talked to one of the employees who was not a family member.

"What's going on?" I asked. "I'm getting this and that in the media, but they never seem to be happy."

"Well, Howard," the employee explained, "the owner's wife aspires to be a Hollywood actress. She wants to be in gossip columns. Do that for her and see what happens."

I did exactly that. I got her name all over the gossip columns, and my life changed. Suddenly I had a happy client. Maybe she couldn't come right out and say these were her goals, but we publicists aren't mind readers—we can only go on what we are told. So it's very good to be utterly honest with your publicist. The goal you don't mention is the goal that your publicity is likely not to reach. It's like therapy—if you don't tell the truth to your therapist, it's hard to make anything real happen in the sessions.

Those are examples of clear goals and hidden goals. What happens if a group has conflicting goals? Nothing good, as the following story indicates. A group of Hollywood celebrities and some very successful businesspeople came to my office because they had an idea for a Web-based business that they believed would be a great financial success. One of the senior people in the group had started a very important Web site and was already very wealthy as a result. The trouble began when I asked them what their advertising budget was, and they became coy. They wouldn't quote me an exact figure. If I don't know what you're spending on advertising, it's awfully hard for me to put together an appropriate PR budget for you.

Then I asked them what kind of public relations budget

they were thinking about for launching the site. If it's somewhere between $30,000 and $50,000 a month, I can do a pretty nice media campaign. If we go up higher, to the $150,000 to $250,000 a month range, we can start thinking about special events, mailings, and other ways of attracting attention. If these individuals were looking to make a very big bet on this business, then perhaps they would be willing to step up and create the appropriate public relations campaign. Instead of providing an answer, they began to argue, right there in my office, about what their goals were, about what they really wanted to accomplish, and about what path would accomplish their goals. I respectfully withdrew from consideration. It's tough enough to satisfy a client who knows what he wants, but to satisfy a group with conflicting desires and goals? That's an impossibility.

People sometimes ask me, "How much does PR cost?" I answer with a question—"How much does a car cost?"

Those are your three options—clear goals, murky goals, or conflicting goals. Which do you think is likely to get you the most traction in your campaign?

Now let's talk about how you measure your PR—how you compare the press and results you're getting with the goals (clear to you and clearly conveyed to your publicist, I hope) that you initially set. At a bare minimum, a public relations campaign has to pay for itself. But you didn't go to all the trouble of creating a PR campaign in order to break even. You went in looking for specific results. Are you achieving them?

First of all, let's measure the press side of the equation. The success of PR is measured in terms of batting average. You don't hit a home run with every single call to every single journalist. If I've got a great story to tell and I call five journalists, I might end up with two or three stories. And that's not bad. If I haven't got such a great story to tell, my office might have to contact a hundred journalists before we get a single piece running anywhere. How about you? If you've been following the recipe in this book, you matched your messages to the right media. As a result, your batting average doesn't have to be 1.000 for you to have a very successful campaign. In how many places has your story appeared? How positive have the mentions been? Did you have a photo in some or all of the stories? Have journalists come back to you for your opinion, now that you are an expert in their minds in a given field? So that's the first thing you want to measure—are you getting noticed in the media in the ways that you desire?

Now let's talk about results. What are the specific results that you intended for your campaign? Perhaps it's simply more sales. Are your numbers up? Can you attribute the increase in your numbers specifically to your PR campaign, or were there other things you were doing, such as increasing your advertising, that might deserve the credit? The easiest way to determine this is to ask your new customers how they heard about you. Was it from an article or from an ad? Don't be surprised if people think that they saw an article about you in one place when it actually appeared in the other. The important thing isn't that they remember exactly where they read about you, or even what they read about you. The important thing is that they came into your place of business waving a credit card at you. That's what you want to measure.

Perhaps your goal was not simply to get more customers or clients on the same financial level as you've had in the past. Maybe you wanted to sell into a new marketplace. The margins are often higher when you are selling more expensive goods, such as a luxury car or a custom home. Perhaps you're a car dealer and you want to move more Range Rovers than economy cars, because the margins are bigger on those expensive imports. Or maybe you are a home builder looking to move away from middle-class tract housing and into an upscale market where you can charge more, and make more, on each house. Are you getting what you wanted? Are you able to sell into that new market? Are you making more sales of big-ticket items with those delightfully higher margins? It shouldn't be too hard for you to figure that out. If you don't take the time to determine where your new sales or better quality of sales are coming from, you'll never know if your campaign worked. A little bit of pulse taking is essential.

Let's say you had a different goal—you wanted to create some national attention for your business so that you could find either a buyer of the business or a franchiser who might be interested in franchising your business across the country or across the world. Here, the measure of success is not simply whether you got your name in the paper or increased sales at your in-town location. The real question is whether your phone is ringing and potential buyers or potential franchisers are making the call. In other words, judge your campaign in terms of the specific results that you sought when you started the campaign. Don't let getting in the press become an end in and of itself. Ultimately, press is great, but results matter. That's the third definition of PR.

What happens if you're *not* getting the results you sought? Adversity is often a greater teacher than success. Just because you're not getting the desired results doesn't mean your campaign is a failure. Here's a for-instance: Academy Award–winning film producer Cathy Schulman and filmmaker Ted Braun created a documentary called *Darfur Now*. We got the movie a front-page story in the Calendar section of the *Los Angeles Times*. You can't ask for much more than that, especially for an independent film, a documentary, and one about a pretty sobering topic at that. The film was screened at only one theater in Los Angeles, and unfortunately, it did poorly at that theater.

What about in New York? The film got a glowing review in the *New York Times* but did poorly in theaters there too. Was their investment in public relations a waste of money? No. They learned something important: if you get on the front page of the Calendar section and you still can't fill a theater in Los Angeles, and if you get a great review in the *New York Times* and you fare no better in the Big Apple, then you learned that you've got a topic that people just may not be ready to deal with. More important, you learned that you did everything you could to get your message about the movie out there. Would it have made sense for them to continue to spend money publicizing the film? Absolutely not. They learned that they had taken it as far as they could, and that sort of lesson, no matter how painful, is vital if one is to be realistic about where to invest one's time and money.

In an earlier chapter, I mentioned a real estate company that was launched in the real estate recession of 2007. We began the campaign with an approach that sought to draw interest to the company based on its position as a contrarian. Who would be crazy enough to start a real estate company in a bad market like this? It's a neat story, but when real estate is down, nobody wants to read—or write—about real estate. We didn't get the size or quality of the stories we originally sought. If you aren't getting the P out of the equation—the press—it's awfully hard to get the R side, the results. So it was time to retool. We decided to go with the creation of a "noncontroversial controversy," the topic explained in a previous chapter.

We created an op-ed for them to run along the lines of, "How we realtors are to blame for today's market." No self-respecting realtor would ever blame himself for a down market. There are too many other convenient whipping boys—the Federal Reserve, the subprime lending crisis, the price of gasoline, the fact that the USC football team hasn't won a national championship in two whole years. But the last thing a realtor would ever do is look in the mirror and say, "It's my fault." That's exactly why we chose this contrarian approach. By creating a noncontroversial controversy, we were able to stir things up, garner attention for our client, and keep our client in the news for more than just a day. The twin lessons of Darfur and the real estate company are these: If you aren't getting press, you can't get results, so change what you're doing with regard to getting press. And, if you're getting press but you aren't getting results, it might just be time to stick a fork in it.

Chances are, though, that your messages are a lot more upbeat than the tragic story of Darfur, and that the business or cultural environment in which you are operating is much more successful than the depressed real estate market that exists as I am writing these words. Since that's the case, the chances are good that your well-thought-out, well-executed public relations campaign is achieving for you some, most, or even all of the goals you've set for it (and conveyed clearly to your publicist), not to go overboard repeating that point. In that case, it's time to break out the bubbly, toast the success of your venture, and celebrate. But as Cervantes wrote, "The road is better than the inn." In other words, we're always happiest pursuing a goal instead of attaining it. That's the paradoxical nature of the human mind. Now it's time to ask ourselves not just what we have achieved, but where do we want to go from here? Now that our initial goals have been reached, what do we have to do to keep on track toward our overall goal? That's the subject of our next chapter.

CHAPTER 14

USING THE MEDIA— SO IT DOESN'T USE YOU

T his chapter is all about consuming the media you want to use . . . before it consumes you. You've got to know how to play the media game, because it's so easy to get played by the media. In the Billy Wilder movie *Ace in the Hole*, Kirk Douglas plays Chuck Tatum, a newspaper reporter with negligible morals who says, "Bad news sells best because good news is no news." They made that movie in 1951. Nothing's changed.

It's tough to be a star today. There's no wall separating the public and the private, and stars find their privacy violated in unimaginable ways. It's not surprising that stars can lose their temper and display bad behavior. Even stars who have learned to use the media instead of being used by it can still find themselves on the wrong end of the publicity equation.

In today's world, the paparazzi will yell stars' kids' names out as they're going to school. It's a little terrifying when the media knows who your kids are, what they look like, and where their school is located. You'd get upset too.

Today, there's an especially irksome Web site called Gawker. com with a feature called the Gawker Stalker. If you see a celebrity, you're supposed to e-mail or text them and let them know where you are and what you're seeing. The problem is that this is a great way to alert people who want to become famous by killing celebrities in order to have their names associated with them, à la John Lennon or Rebecca Schaeffer. This isn't a "what if" or esoteric issue—this is a "When might it happen next?" issue. As I write these words, a young man has killed eight people in a public place, injured scores more, and turned the gun on himself, and in his suicide note he wrote, "Now I'm famous." If shooting eight people will make you famous for, dare I say, fifteen minutes, what about shooting celebrities you find via Gawker Stalker or some similar means? Jimmy Kimmel spoke for most people in Hollywood when, in his role as substitute host on *Larry King Live*, he told a spokesperson for Gawker Stalker, "I would hate to see you arriving in hell and someone sending a text message saying, 'Guess who's here.'"

The paparazzi make the counterargument that we live in a capitalistic society, that what they do is legal, and that they're simply making a living. Their attitude is that if you don't like what we're doing, change the law; but they're still protected by the First Amendment. These are powerful examples of how the media uses celebrities, even to the point of putting their lives at risk.

Sometimes celebrities have nobody to blame but themselves. We love to criticize celebrities who get involved in politics by saying that they don't know what they're talking about, and that they should stick to reading lines. Half the time, that's true. Many celebrities who become involved in politics are ill-informed and ill-prepared, and they've overestimated the tolerance of the public for their tendentious proclamations. Yet celebrities who have figured out how to use the media have big lessons for the rest of us. So what do smart celebrities know that the rest of us don't?

The first thing they do before they appear or consent to an interview is to find out exactly what that show or reporter is all about. I once received a call from Chelsea Handler requesting my client's presence on *Chelsea Lately*, her popular E! show. I called my client and asked her if she had seen the show. She said she hadn't seen it, so I suggested that she record it and see how comfortable she feels with it, to determine whether it was the right forum for her. She watched the show and decided it made sense for her to appear on it.

If you don't watch the show, you're at a disadvantage from the start. Let's look at Larry King. His staff says that they give people a chance to express their own views. Larry isn't Bill O'Reilly or even his network mate Lou Dobbs. Larry King knows himself—he's as comfortable with Dick Cheney as he is with Hillary Rodham Clinton. He may ask a tough question, but he's never going to ask too mean a question, and as a result, people feel very comfortable going on his show. Before *you* go on any interview show—local, national, or a cable show taped in the host's basement—watch it a bunch of times and make sure it really is a good venue for you and for your message. Nothing looks worse than a liberal finding himself grilled on a conservative show, or vice versa. People really should know better.

Steven Colbert turned the gentle White House Press Corps Dinner into a roast of President Bush. The next year it was hosted by Rich Little. Enough said about knowing your audiences?

Chances are, there's a host of media that you never read because it doesn't reflect your political viewpoint. Most of us don't bother with TV networks, newspapers, or magazines with which we don't generally agree. It's just too infuriating, and besides, who has time? But if you're going to be a public figure in your community, it really will be worth your time to keep up with all of the publications that might cover you, not just the ones with which you feel ideologically compatible.

The *Village Voice* is the granddaddy of all "alternative" urban newspapers, and outlets like the *Chicago Reader, L.A. Weekly*, and others have followed in its illustrious footsteps. If you're an environmental activist, you might pick up those papers every week. But if you're a local developer, you might not. If so, it's time to make a change. Read it and know how they're going to cover you—or criticize you—so that you can be prepared if and when they call.

I mentioned the show *Chelsea Lately* on E!. Celebrities don't always love E!, because it tends toward the salacious at times. You may not want someone doing a "true Hollywood story" on you—but if you're a celebrity, you darned well want to know how they cover celebs should you one day be in their sights.

Every talk show has its own purpose and theme. Geraldo Rivera, for example, is a rabble-rouser. His show is not so much oriented on the left/right scale as it is in terms of creating excitement. Geraldo says, "Give me an issue, and I'll grab it like a dog holding a tennis ball."

Oprah, "the Queen," is about enlightenment and empowerment, especially for women. She is the closest thing we have to royalty in this country. She has taken the concepts of enlightenment and empowerment and built them into not just a TV show or a magazine but a superpowerful international brand. Note that these ideas are not new, but it took someone like an Oprah—it *specifically* took Oprah—to turn them into an inspirational brand. People love her, and what happened to Martha Stewart could most likely never happen to her. Oprah has such a large reservoir of goodwill that the public would never stand for a prosecutor going after her on some sort of nitpicking charge, whether related to financial markets or anything else.

Dr. Phil is about redemption. My friend Pat O'Brien went on *Dr. Phil* after a troubled period in his life. I suggested that Pat watch a whole lot of *Dr. Phil* beforehand. Pat got the message; it doesn't matter how wonderful you are, because if you go on *Dr. Phil*, you'll spend the first forty-five minutes of the show with Dr. Phil taking you to the woodshed. The good news is that in the last segment, Dr. Phil will redeem you.

And that's exactly what happened with Pat. It was forty-five minutes of getting spanked on national television, and then fifteen minutes of Dr. Phil saying, "I know you. I know your son. You're a good man and you made a mistake." And that's Dr. Phil's brand of redemption. We actually like that. Dr. Phil expresses the widely held point of view in our society that we are a little too easy on people, we don't hold people to high enough standards, and as a result, they fall. Dr. Phil took the idea of redemption and quite successfully turned it into a brand.

When you go on *Dr. Phil*, you know it's not going to be fun for those first forty-five minutes, but there will be a light at the end of the tunnel. I've seen noncelebrities go on *Dr. Phil* who had done something pretty outrageous, violent, or even incestuous. Dr. Phil asks them his famous question, "What were you thinking?" But when I'm sitting and watching the show, I'm thinking, "What were you thinking, going on this show? Have you watched it? You may get out of it at the end, but it certainly won't be a good time." Not for Pat O'Brien; not for anyone.

Ellen DeGeneres is about originality and freshness. When I book a guest on her show, I never know what kind of scenario they will come up with, but I do know it will be fresh and original and something uniquely Ellen.

Next up: Regis and Kelly. Their show is pure entertainment— the old-fashioned coffee klatch. Notice what time the show is on—nine A.M. Notice who goes on it—likeable celebrities. And notice the homey, almost throwback nature of the set and the props. It's almost purposely low-tech, unslick by design. Let's say something bad happens in the news. Regis and Kelly will shake their heads, grimace appropriately, and then move on to Kelly's latest cute story about her son Joaquin. They don't spend a lot of time in the dark places. We like the comfort of knowing with whom we're having coffee in the morning. When Regis and Kelly choose guest hosts, they choose celebrities in the same vein as themselves—the Howie Mandels, the Mario Lopezes, the Pat Sajaks of the world, people who are the same brand and essence. That's what their audiences have come to expect.

We don't expect Regis and Kelly to suddenly turn into Dr. Phil and start asking hard questions. We don't expect Lou Dobbs to ask bad guys bent on destroying the middle class how they're enjoying their summer. We hate it when we see a movie billed as a comedy and it turns out to be some heart-wrenching drama.

It's the same thing when we watch our favorite interview shows—we know what to expect, consciously or subconsciously, and we pretty much get it every time. Since that's the case, you ought to be very clear about what you're getting yourself into anytime you think about appearing on a show.

You might be thinking, I'm not likely to get on *Regis and Kelly*. That may or may not be true, but you don't want to make the mistake of assuming that all local news or interview shows are the same. Each has its own different ideological and political bent. In local markets, those differences may be more nuanced than on national news shows, but you've got to be aware of the direction they favor. The hardest thing for me to figure out is what radio or television station to place a celebrity on for an interview if I don't really know the market. I don't want to put my clients on conservative shows where they'll be attacked for being liberal, and vice versa. I'm always amazed at how often the wrong person is on the wrong show for the wrong reason. I always want to ask: what are you doing there? If you have a choice between being on an important show that you know nothing about or doing no media at all, just say no. It's just not worth it.

What happens when the media attacks you? You don't have to take it. Jennifer Love Hewitt is an actress and TV star I've known for more than twenty years. She and her fiancé went on a getaway and TMZ published an unflattering picture of her behind, which, unfortunately, ended up on the cover of *People* magazine. Well, Jennifer struck back. "I'm not fat," she told the news media. "A size two isn't fat. I'm a real woman, and like every woman, I say, love your body. I will not have one photo from a paparazzo define me."

The consensus from the media: she did the right thing. After all, Jennifer Love Hewitt had some pretty serious money in the bank when it came to credibility and a good name. She was a spokesperson for Hanes, as down-to-earth a product as you can find in America, for goodness' sake. She earned her right to say what she said, and we loved her for it.

The media loves trends. I love trends, because they're easy to market. Let's talk about our friend the local environmental activist. In addition to providing her own set of facts to the media, she should also provide a list of credible people who can be interviewed for the story and their phone numbers. Think beyond yourself. If you've got a great list of people for the journalist to contact, you're going to get a longer and better story. And next time around, who's the journalist going to consider as the major expert or guide to great contacts? You, of course.

Earlier, I discussed Spiegel's move from polyester items to becoming the "new" Neiman-Marcus catalog. We had a very aggressive media campaign to complement their focus as a direct marketer. Our goal was to upgrade the image of the company, secure new customers, break down the resistance of the fashion editors toward "a catalog, God forbid," and let the business community know that Spiegel was a new company and one they should be doing business with. As a result of all the efforts of the many people working on their behalf, I received numerous calls from people saying, "We hear Spiegel's really hot."

"Absolutely," I told them, and I gave them the story. Then I gave them the phone number of my friend Roberta Maneker at the Direct Marketing Association, and told them that she could talk about the whole world of hot catalogs and Spiegel's place in it. Sure enough, they would call her, and the story would be even better. Don't you think a story about you will be a better story, from your perspective, if you get to choose everyone else the reporter interviews? (Well, you don't get to choose everyone, but you sure get to have a lot of influence if you can save the journalist a few steps.) Conversely, if people called Roberta at the Direct Marketing Association to ask about catalogs, she'd say, "Why don't you call Howard Bragman? He represents Spiegel, and Spiegel is a wonderful example of what you're talking about." We became the best one-two punch since Batman and Robin.

The media also loves "ten tips." The media loves anything you can quantify, in fact. If you put out a press release with Ten Tips for Staying Healthy This Holiday Season, they'll eat it up.

If you're that environmental dry cleaner, you might have "Ten Easy Tips for Becoming Environmentally Aware at Home." This shows you really care and that you're the leader in this trend.

When do you start talking to the media? Before you need them. Build relationships with the media before you need stories about you, the same way you have insurance before your home burns down. If you're launching something new, whether it's a business, an idea, or a campaign of any sort, build the political relationships ahead of time. The first time you should be talking to the media is before you pitch them, or, worse, criticize them for a story that has appeared somewhere.

One of the tools we use with the media is a pitch letter. Whether it goes by messenger, snail mail, or e-mail, the concept is the same: the letter is one page, laying out what you're selling.

Keep it simple and brief. There's a classic five-paragraph rhythm to such letters: the introduction—I'm Joe Shmoe and I want to tell you about a revolutionary concept that's going to change your life; the second paragraph introduces your client, your product, your idea, and the timing; the third paragraph is the heart of the pitch—it's affordable, it's groundbreaking, it's revolutionary—the true attributes; in the fourth paragraph you're winding down and you lay out all of the virtues—why the world should care, why you should put this on your show, and so on; the fifth is the "thank you for your time and consideration" and the next steps. Pitch letters and e-mails should almost never exceed one page.

I've been at this a long time, and I rarely accept a "no" from the media. That's because in my mind, "no" really means "not right now." But I have planted a seed. It might not be sprouting just yet, but it will. I'll keep it watered and fertilized, and eventually that flower—that wonderful story I want—will bloom.

Sometimes I even put negative things out about my client if they aren't too negative, if they're "old news," and if my client approves, because it gives me credibility. It shows that I'm not a Pollyanna about my clients—that I know there are two sides to some issues. I'd rather create a sense of balance myself than wonder what the media is going to dig up about my client. Along these lines, it's very important to remember that new bad news is worse than old bad news. It's much better for a politician to say, "I smoked pot in the seventies" and let the story appear and get buried than have the *New York Times* discover it—or, worse still, release it—the night before the election. Another rule of thumb about managing your relations with the media: you can't push hard all the time. Sometimes you want to let the media discover a story. If you've got something new and exciting going on at your store, build word-of-mouth, and let them come to you.

Quotations are a crucially important way to get your message out. A good quote will be, well, quoted—that is, picked up by other publications and media outlets. A bad quote dies. Don't be dull. Don't use the word "thrilled," as it is the most hackneyed and overused quote in quotedom. Do be visual, fun, and memorable. You'll see it gets a lot more traction. A friend of mine wrote a book about when people first knew their sexual orientation, called *When I Knew*. I said, "I knew I was gay when the favorite part of my bar mitzvah was working with the party planner." That quote was on the back cover of the book; it was used in *People*, *Newsweek*, *Variety*, and on *Oprah*. Now those are legs.

Finally, media begets media. When one of my clients was named Bachelor of the Month in *Cosmopolitan* magazine, we worked out a four-page spread about it in *Esquire*. Parlay what you've got into bigger stories using the tools we have discussed. You don't necessarily have to be afraid of the media. It's a voracious beast, but it can be tamed to some degree. Make it your friend, feed it when it's hungry, don't run from it lest it think you have something to hide, and then let it go out and devour your competitor. How does that sound?

CHAPTER 15

PRESS AGENTRY, SUPPRESS AGENTRY, AND OPPRESS AGENTRY:
A PRIMER

Media relations involves specialized techniques. If what you're doing isn't working, then try something new. This chapter is for you. As a publicist, I have three basic roles: press agentry, where I'm trying to get a story about a client into the media; suppress agentry, where I'm trying to keep a story about a client *out* of the media; and oppress agentry, where we proactively go after people who are actively doing bad things to our client. In order to understand what I do as a publicist, you must first understand what these three activities are and how they work.

Often, clients come to me and tell me the kind of story they'd like to see in the newspaper or on TV. My challenge is to find a delicate way (they're paying the bills, after all) to let them know that the story that they have suggested can't work. For a story to attract the attention of the media, it has to have a "hook"—something appealing, innovative, and exciting. It's got to be fresh, because you won't find a more jaded group of people than the news media, and especially the media that covers celebrities. It's also got to be a story that actually belongs in the media in the first place—not everything is newsworthy or attention-getting. Similarly, a story cannot be too subtle for the media, which often wields its power with bludgeonlike force. If you're pushing a champagne that has just been introduced from the 1999 stock, for example, that may be hard to get placed, except in some very specialized wine publications, because it's not big news to the general public. So how do you get a story like that into the paper? Why not throw a "Party Like It's 1999 Party" in honor of the introduction? Free champagne for the media? Now you've got a chance. If you can't get any media coverage for your story, it doesn't matter what your message is.

Press Agentry

Press agentry harkens back to the late 1800s and the early 1900s, the birth of contemporary communications. The most classic example of early day press agentry is the circus coming to town. There's nothing more traditional than the circus—it's really the same story every year. So how do you get people excited about something that doesn't really hold any surprises? And how do you draw attention to a story like this even if the local press isn't inclined to cover it?

There are two ways. You can come in by train in the middle of the night and quietly set up your tent, and hope that people buy tickets. Or you can have a circus parade down Main Street with lions, tigers, and acrobats thrilling the residents of the town. This creates a buzz—everybody in the community will start asking each other, "Did you see what happened on Main Street today?"

Gene Autry, the first owner of the Angels baseball team, used to say that his happiest childhood memories were of those circus parades marching down Main Street of his hometown Tioga, Texas. He even chose the bright red color that symbolizes the Angels because that was the color of the circus that came to his Tioga—and he always remembered the joy he and his friends experienced, symbolized by that bright red. In other words, a well-told media story can last forever.

Even today, circuses are great at press agentry. You can have the local news station paint the weather report on the side of an elephant, as my friend Lynda Knott did in Chicago. You can do just about anything. But the only thing you don't want to do is come into town in the middle of the night and quietly set up your tents. It's true that circuses have been around for more than a century, so there's not much new that you can think of. And yet there's always a great way to spin the story to draw attention to its arrival.

The modern-day spin on the circus parade down Main Street is this: whenever you have something valuable and important to show off and you want to generate a story about it, create the modern equivalent of a parade down Main Street. Whether it's a diamond, a crown, a vintage dress, or an important painting—whatever you've got, bring it to town in a Brinks' truck surrounded by lots of guards, with a police motorcycle escort. It's a fairly standard PR move to create that kind of excitement—and it just about always works.

The goal is to create a story that is practically impossible for the press to ignore. When mogul Marvin Davis opened up the Carnegie Deli in Beverly Hills, his publicists created an event that the media just *had* to attend—they dropped the world's largest matzo ball into the world's largest vat of chicken soup. Actress and celebrity Carol Channing, whose signature song, "Diamonds Are a Girl's Best Friend," symbolized the opulence of Beverly Hills, presided over the event. The opening of a local delicatessen (admittedly in the heart of Beverly Hills) attracted publicity worldwide.

Another way to garner attention is to have somebody do something worthy of a listing in the *Guinness Book of World Records*. Everybody loves the world's largest, the world's longest, the world's greatest, the world's fastest . . . anything. It could be jumping rope. It could be yodeling. It could be anything you think of. For Procter & Gamble, we created the world's largest conga line at Calle Ocho in Miami. At the head of the conga line: Gloria Estefan. No way could the media miss that story.

Even if you don't have the glamour or star power of a Gloria Estefan, you can still use this concept to draw attention. For example, we represented the company that created the salad dressing for Bob's Big Boy, a restaurant chain. How do you draw the media's attention to salad dressing? By creating the world's longest salad bar. Did it work? You better believe it. Another successful media event for Bob's Big Boy was to create a look-alike contest for the iconic, heavyset, smiling Bob—in his red and white checked overalls—perched atop each restaurant in the chain.

Today, we're living in a reality-TV culture. People want to be famous, but they often aren't strategic about what they want to be famous for. I've learned in my career as a publicist that for five hundred or a thousand bucks, you can get people to do almost anything. I've staged at least half a dozen look-alike contests, and they've always drawn the media. In addition to the Bob's Big Boy look-alike contest, we did a contest for dogs and owners who looked the most alike. I'm not sure I'd like to enter a contest like that—my dog is much better looking than I am—but enough people attended that we were able to achieve all the media attention my client could have hoped for.

If you're going to create a public event, go where the people already are. It can take a lot of money and advertising dollars to draw a crowd, so why not go where a crowd can easily form—especially a location that resonates with the message that you are trying to create? For the California Milk Advisory Board, we did a "moo-off" at the Farmers' Market in Los Angeles. Why the Farmers' Market? It draws tons of people every day, so we had a built-in crowd for our event . . . and plenty of people who wanted to moo for a chance at $500. Also, a farmers' market dovetails neatly with the idea of cows and milk. Get it—milking cows and farmers? The media did. The coverage was excellent.

Sometimes it makes sense, though, to avoid the crowds and find a new space for your message. For John McTiernan's film

The Last Action Hero, starring Arnold Schwarzenegger, the studio put the name of the movie on a side of a rocket ship. They were the first ones to do such a thing, taking press agentry to a place where man had never gone before. Space isn't a crowded place for ads, so they were able to draw worldwide attention. Be outrageous in your quest for publicity.

Another important tool in press agentry is to think about who your friends are and how they can help. When I represented Anheuser-Busch, which markets, among other brands, Budweiser beer, they were opening a new warehouse in Chicago, and our goal was to attract mainstream media. This is the kind of story that typically lends itself to a small squib in the business section—"New Warehouse Opens, Creating 200 New Jobs." Not too much sizzle there. To make a bigger splash, I hired a friend of mine, Kathy Byrne, to cater the opening. It just so happened that Kathy's mother was a woman named Jane Byrne, and Jane Byrne at that time happened to be the first female mayor of the city of Chicago. With Kathy on board, we had a very good chance of getting the mayor to come as well. But even with the mayor present, what could you do to jazz up the opening of a beer warehouse?

How about this: six skydivers with different Anheuser-Busch brand logos on their parachutes landing at the warehouse, which was surrounded by a wall of ice. The mayor and August Busch III crushed the ice with pickaxes—as cameras rolled—and suddenly the world-famous Clydesdale horses emerged from the warehouse.

Big news.

Another rule of thumb for publicists: if you can't dazzle them with brilliance, use your imagination (okay, what I really mean is, baffle them with bullshit). Anheuser-Busch was trying to get publicity for its new ad campaign featuring commentator and oddsmaker Jimmy the Greek. So I came up with an event to get some media attention—a luncheon, to which we invited the top sports journalists and their crews. Jimmy the Greek came, along with a famous psychic and *Playboy's* resident prognosticator Anson Mount, and all present were invited to "Beat the

Greek"—to come up with predictions that were even more accurate than Jimmy's. There were Anheuser-Busch products for the best pickers. If you think the media didn't respond to an offer of free beer, then you don't understand the media.

Actually, understanding the media is critical to getting coverage of your story or event. You have to think like a journalist, which means that you must create something that fits into their idea of a story that they can put in the newspaper or on the air. If you're pitching a TV story, you've got to say, "Here are the visuals. Here's the hook." As a society, we're becoming more visual every day, and an increasing number of people receive their information through interactive media, rather than through print or radio. So you've got to be outrageous visually. Outrageous is a good place to be—it's not a bad thing.

During my PR career I have proudly represented a number of controversial people and issues. If I had done it once, people would say, "Howard's gone off his rocker." Since I have a history of it, they now say, "That's just Howard."

Speaking of outrageous, if you've ever spent any time in Los Angeles, then you might have seen one of our local icons, Angeline. She is a blonde-haired (okay, I'm giving her the benefit of the doubt), busty personality of indeterminate age who rolls around town in a pink Corvette. If you don't know who she is, Google her; she's unique. She always dresses the same and always looks the same—she has a brand and she lives up to it. She's made a life for herself by being outrageous in a town where outrageous sells. How old exactly is Angeline? We never want to guess the age of a lady, but she was born somewhere between the advent of the La Brea Tar Pits and the first hit single of Britney Spears.

I mention Angeline because we brought her in for a red carpet event we put together to create publicity for a coffee table book of photographs that depicted *A Day in the Life of Hollywood*. At that event, one of the reporters had the effrontery to ask Angeline, "What's it like to be the ultimate wannabe in Hollywood?"

At first she looked hurt and a little shocked. She was certainly not used to this sort of rough treatment. Her image has landed her in a bunch of movies, appearances, and who knows what else over the years, but she rarely came in contact with tough questions from reporters. To her credit, Angeline recovered quickly.

"I'm not a wannabe," she said. "I'm an I am."

Angeline is exactly right—in the minds of the media and the millions of people who have seen her in movies or on TV, she *is*; she represents a fantasy Southern California lifestyle: big boobs, blond hair, pink Corvette, and all. And no one can take that away from her.

Richard Simmons, Larry King, and the late Minnie Pearl all understood the importance of their own appearance as their "brand." When you see them, you know it's them. Minnie Pearl always appeared on stage at the Grand Ole Opry with price tags hanging from her thrift store purchases, and her fans loved her for it. Larry King is always wearing those suspenders. And if Richard Simmons showed up with a haircut and a nice suit instead of his trademark shorts and tank top, would we recognize him as Mr. "Sweatin' to the Oldies"? Doubtful.

When it comes to creating a personal brand, Halloween queen Elvira has the best gig in show business. She makes millions working a few weeks a year because everyone associates her fiercely attractive look with Halloween. Nice work if you can get it. Similarly, Bruce Vilanch has won Emmys for writing the scripts for the Academy Awards shows. (Yes, they really do have scripts.) Don't believe for a second that your favorite Hollywood celebrities are capable of tossing off bon mots and great jokes that they just thought up while being fitted for those $50,000 dresses or tuxedos. Vilanch became famous to tens of millions of television viewers as the fat guy with the stringy blond hair and red glasses on *Hollywood Squares*.

If you're going to talk about creating a personal image, then we can't possibly omit Dennis Rodman, who has perfected outrageousness by his looks, wedding dresses, and antics on and off the basketball court just to get a buzz going. Rodman was known to basketball aficionados as perhaps the greatest rebounder in the history of the game, but he was not a "first name" athlete, like a Michael (Jordan, for those of you under thirty) or a Tiger. And then he spent an evening with Madonna, who told him all about the importance of outrageousness as a means for self-promotion. And suddenly Dennis Rodman was as famous (or infamous) an athlete as American society has ever seen.

Many basketball players capitalize on their images in the media as "players"—expensive house, nice car, lots of women. Doug and Jackie Christie—one of the NBA's most notorious couples—however, have turned this notion on its head to create their own brand based on monogamy and fidelity; even the title of their television show, *Committed*, and their book, *No Ordinary Love* reinforce this image. Their dedication and commitment to one another has created controversy in the media in such instances where Jackie disapproved of Doug speaking with female reporters or stood up for him during squirmishes on the court. This hype simply reinforces the message of their unique and personal brand of celebrity fidelity.

You don't have to be a basketball player to get press, though. A smart way for any person or business to create publicity is to find "qualifiers" that make your story unique. If you can be the first, the most expensive, or the biggest, or anything along those lines, you'll attract the media spotlight. Here, we're taking a relatively meaningless fact or situation and spinning it into gossamer. As an example, in the early 1990s, I worked with the team that created the Peninsula Hotel in Beverly Hills. This was a newsworthy story, simply because this was the first Peninsula Hotel outside Hong Kong, and the first new hotel to be built in Beverly Hills in twenty-five years. My fear was that we would only get a short business story in the *Los Angeles Times* Business section—"Construction to Begin" or "Franchise Awarded." It doesn't get any more boring than that. So how do you publicize this into something even greater?

The management team took me to the land on which the

hotel would be built. It was two or three acres, and getting that much contiguous space in Beverly Hills was not an easy feat.

"That's quite a piece of land," I told them.

They nodded knowingly.

"We've been putting this parcel together for a few years," they told me.

"What's it worth?" I asked, sensing an angle.

"Something like fifty million an acre," they told me. Back then, that was a lot . . . for a lot. And suddenly the story came to me. I called media outlets and told them that they had the opportunity to take a photo of the most valuable two-acre lot "west of the Mississippi." Why west of the Mississippi? It just sounds better when you put some sort of intriguing limitation on it. That AP news photo of a vacant lot in Beverly Hills—and the name of the Peninsula Hotel—flashed all around the world.

Finding the story in a seemingly mundane event is the true art of press agentry. Take the Las Vegas Hilton, which hired us to draw attention to its sports book. Not much of a story there, because every hotel in town has a sports book—those luxurious lounges where you place your bets on anything from golf to mixed martial arts. So what could make the one at the Las Vegas Hilton different and compelling?

The Academy Award season was just getting underway when we began working on this assignment. So we went to the head oddsmaker of the Las Vegas Hilton's sports book and worked with him to create odds for the Oscars. You can't bet on the Oscars at the Las Vegas Hilton, or anywhere else in America, as far as I know. At least not legally. But we certainly got a great story out of it. Creating a "line" for the Oscars wasn't a moneymaker for the Las Vegas Hilton . . . but it certainly was an attention gotter.

Sometimes we reach back into our clients' lives to find ways to have them connect with new audiences. Sheila Kuehl, a popular political activist, was running for California state representative. Today, she is a highly respected and powerful member of the state senate, but this was her first foray into elective office. It just so happened that Sheila Kuehl, prior to her political career, had been an actress (where have we ever heard that before?). She was a member of the cast of the hit sitcom *The Lives and Loves of Dobie Gillis*. We put together a "Dobie Gillis cast reunion" that drew national attention and actually received coverage in *People* magazine. At first, her handlers were suspicious.

"What do we want *People* magazine for?" they asked—a question I thought was rather shortsighted. "Her district is West L.A."

"People in West L.A. read *People* magazine," I reminded them. "Not just the *L.A. Times*." And you can count on the fact that none of her opponents were able to attract attention from *People* magazine. Sheila's new political career was off and running—she won.

The key to press agentry: never settle for a boring or mundane story about an event or situation to which you want to attract attention. Outrageousness, creativity, and appealing to the media's sense of fun are surefire ways to get the attention you want. And never forget that you can find people to do just about anything for five hundred bucks.

Suppress Agentry

One of the most important jobs of media relations people is to keep things about a client out of the press that can be embarrassing, potentially volatile, or inaccurate. Or maybe you just want to release the information on your own terms. If a story is released too soon, it can ruin a public relations strategy. Unfortunately, if you're a celebrity, you don't have to give the media permission to write about you. You can't "officially" stop them. In this country, we have a constitutionally guaranteed freedom of the press. You have to accept the fact that they're going to write about you, but you don't have to participate in the story. Yes, you can sue them if you believe a story to be libelous or slanderous, but that just keeps the story alive in the media even longer. And for legal reasons, it's practically impossible for a person in the public eye to win that kind of case. You can *suggest* that the media not write about you, but you can't stop them if they're determined to put out that story.

There's a concept called "scorched earth." If someone in high places doesn't like you, they'll do all the opposition research on you and turn you from a hero to pariah quicker than you can say Dan Rather. This is a situation where someone is trying actively to destroy your reputation. Consider Valerie Plame, who was "outed" as a CIA agent. It can be a White House strategy, a corporate strategy, and it's sometimes a Hollywood strategy. Before you think about adopting a scorched earth policy, be careful, because karma will come around and bite you in the butt. You can easily get a reputation as a bad person. You better have played this game for a long time before you step into the scorched earth arena.

Keep in mind that if someone's doing a negative story about you, freedom of the press does *not* mean that you have to talk to them. I have in my possession a famous tape of former Supreme Court chief justice Warren Burger knocking to the ground an expensive TV camera and snarling, "Get that thing out of my face." If it's okay for a chief justice of the Supreme Court not to participate in a media story, it's okay for the rest of us.

If the media is concocting a damaging story about you, things may be much worse if you cooperate with the media. One of the most perplexing questions of modern times is why people who have done something wrong willingly participate in stories on exposé shows like *60 Minutes*. Anytime you cooperate with the media, the story will be longer and juicier. Sometimes the right thing to do is to respond with a statement. The last thing you may want is your face plastered all over TV news and the Internet, responding to charges in a way that makes you look bad.

A recent example of this is Floyd Landis, who was stripped of his 2006 Tour de France victory because of a positive drug test after one of the stages of the race. Landis was ill-prepared for the media onslaught that began from the moment the story broke. The way he answered questions from the media made it sound as though he was shifting between many different explanations for the positive drug test—which served to seal the fate of public opinion against him. He lacked a coordinated media strategy and never really got his side of the story out to the public. It may well have been that the French were determined to punish any American who dared to win yet another Tour de France after the humiliation of Lance Armstrong winning a record seven in a row. So the outcome of Landis's case might not have changed, even if he had the greatest "suppress agentry" team on his side. But you never know.

Similarly, one of my clients, a famous actor, was accused of sexual improprieties. First we denied it, but then our lawyers stepped in and made clear to us that if we didn't win this case quickly in the court of public opinion, we would have a much harder time winning it in a court of law. So the question became "How do we respond?" Since the story wasn't true, we decided to get out in front of it and deny it. We didn't do it with a news conference, which would have been conducted in front of a potentially hostile and combative media that's always looking to "make its bones" by trashing a celebrity. Instead, we instructed our client to write a letter to his fans on his MySpace page: "There have been some things said about me," he told his loyal fans, "and they're not true. You know me—you know my history. You know I'm not capable of doing this kind of thing."

The message initially went to his loyal fan base, and then the media ran with the story. Obviously, you can put things in a letter to fans that you can't tell the jaded media. It turned out that the MySpace page was the perfect way to attack the charges and diffuse the situation. His first appeal for clemency was not to the media but to his fans, with whom he already had a positive relationship. You can have a different kind of dialogue in that setting. Marshall McLuhan wrote decades ago that "the medium is the message." In the era of TMZ.com, YouTube.com, and social networking on the Internet, it's still true.

Another approach to suppress agentry is to simply avoid

talking to the "tabloids," either the ones you see in the super-market checkout line, like the *National Enquirer* or the *Weekly World News*, or the online ones such as TMZ.com and PerezHilton.com. Often, having any contact at all with these outlets only gives a dying story more oxygen. Indeed, sometimes the best approach is silence.

A classic example of this is the story of a doctor who was referred to me by Bernie Lewinsky, father of Monica Lewinsky, who herself was the subject of so much notoriety during the Clinton White House years. Bernie's friend was a physician in a volatile marriage to a highly unstable woman. The couple got into an argument. She pulled a gun and murdered three of the children and tried to shoot herself. She survived to face capital murder charges. The doctor, deeply anguished, came to me for advice about how to handle the situation in the media. His youngest son, who survived the attack, lived only because the doctor's wife did not know how to reload her weapon. He now had expenses, trials, trauma—a lot of bad things going on.

A story like this, of course, is perfect fodder for the "usual suspects" of television shows like *20/20* or *60 Minutes*. I didn't want the doctor to be defined for the rest of his life as "that doctor, the one whose wife killed his kids." He could have been everywhere in the media, asking that his privacy be respected, but I knew the best way to handle the situation was to not be helpful to the media. The less he put himself out in the public eye, the sooner he would be able to get on with his life, if he ever could, once the trial was over.

The case went to trial and his wife was convicted in the three murders and sentenced to death. In keeping with the law of the state in which this took place, my client was given the opportunity to make a "victim's statement" in court. I advised him not to do so, telling him that he would be on every television outlet in the country. He took my advice and did not make a statement. Still, the TV cameras wanted to cover him as he was leaving the courthouse on that last day of the trial. I had done a "pre-trip" through the courthouse to scout out alternative exits.

As the doctor and I left the courtroom and headed down the corridor to the elevator, the TV cameras were trying to get ahead of us in order to get a shot of his face.

We tricked them. I pushed the elevator button and once the elevator arrived I grabbed him and we shot down the stairway. A car was waiting out in front, so there were no face shots, which was a good thing. We were out of there. Obviously, people in his local community knew about it, but the story never entered the national mind-set, even though it had all the elements to do so. It could have been on daytime TV for months. The trial was salacious. She tried to pin horrible things on him. Of course, bad relationships and divorces are tough in the best of times. In a situation like this, "suppress agentry" made the difference between a story that resonated with the national media and a chance for this individual to heal in relative privacy.

Along these lines, there's always that conundrum about celebrities—they do everything they can to become famous, and then once they become famous, they do everything they can to shun the media. I call this the "Coors beer syndrome"—anything that's unavailable becomes more desirable. In the early 1970s, before Coors beer became a national brand, it was hard to find and symbolized the essence of chic. Paul Newman made an appearance at The New School in New York in front of Richard Brown's cutting-edge film class, and Newman sipped on a Coors the whole time. The anguished, thirsty New Yorkers in the audience could only imagine just how good that beer tasted. I remember as a boy trying to get some of that beer for my buddies and myself, on the theory that the rarer the fruit, the sweeter the nectar.

At some point, though, beer is beer. Once Coors became a national brand and was available in every 7-Eleven, it lost its sense of uniqueness and excitement, and it became just another brand to promote. I wonder what Paul Newman would drink today if he were to make another such appearance in New York City. Probably something from his own product line, no doubt— publicity is publicity.

The mystique of celebrity can cut both ways. There's nothing more enticing to the media than a celebrity trying to hide from them. They just love that cat and mouse game, and they're happy to play the role of cat. Or, to switch metaphors, it's the Coors beer syndrome all over again—people want what they can't have. If you're a celebrity and you want the media to get off your tail, ironically the best way to accomplish that is by becoming incredibly accessible to them. Print out your schedule for the coming week. Let them know where to find you. When you get to your car, smile, cooperate. Be friendly. There's nothing more boring to the media than a willing subject. Within a week, they'll be off your tail. Otherwise, you can end up experiencing what happens to Brad and Angelina practically every time they get into a car—the media jumps on the hood and harasses them, giving them all kinds of trouble.

When I say that the celebrity mystique can cut both ways, I mean that you can use it to your advantage. I had a friend in Florida who was an artist with a reputation for being, well, an artist. Often, prospective buyers of his work couldn't even locate him—he was rarely in his studio when he was supposed to be. He was able to capitalize on that bad-boy image and create a mystique and command high prices for his art.

What happens when you know that the media is hot on the trail of a story that you just don't want them to cover? It's not as simple as hiring a press agent to call the *Los Angeles Times* and say, "Take that out." That's not how things work. You can make an argument with the media, however, that runs along the lines of, "I don't think that should be included in the story because . . ." and then you take your best shot.

This approach doesn't always work, though. I once represented two individuals who ran an entertainment company in Hollywood. They never told me that one of them had been convicted of a felony many years earlier. Well, the story came to light. I argued with the *Los Angeles Times* that the event had taken place years ago and was irrelevant to their current careers in the movie industry. And in any event, had he not been caught, the statute of limitations would already have run out. The argument cut no ice, and the story ran with that information. You can't win them all.

As for some of the gossip columnists, a good publicist will have a relationship with them and sometimes be able to make a deal with them: if they keep an item off their column or Web site, you'll feed them something else down the road. This sometimes persuades them to take out a snarky word or a bad photograph. Some publicists, unfortunately, will protect one client by throwing another one under the bus. This is an unethical way to practice our trade.

A good lawyer who knows the tabloids can also be a major asset in suppressing negative stories. If the story is false or unprovable, raising the name Bert Fields, Marty Singer, or Larry Stein (some of the top libel and entertainment attorneys in Los Angeles) can often kill or mitigate a potentially negative story.

The key to suppress agentry is to remember that stories, like fire, require oxygen to stay alive. If there's something happening and you don't want it in the papers, don't fan the flames.

Oppress Agentry

Oppress agentry consists of going after any individual for any reason. The usual reason for oppress agentry is not because you don't like someone; rather, it's because he or she is saying or doing something dangerous and destructive to your client's image or career. Sometimes the key to oppress agentry is letting the other side present its story and then counterpunching with your best argument as to why they are inaccurate or wrong.

Take the case of Roseanne Barr. More than a decade ago, she sued her then–talent agency, Triad, on the grounds that the agency was not acting within the bounds of the law when it was "packaging" TV shows. (When a talent agency packages a show, it takes a commission on the success of the whole show and not just on the salary of the agents. If a TV show is successful, we're talking about a lot of money.)

Roseanne's lawsuit upset the other talent agencies as well, because if agencies were denied the right to package shows, they stood to lose hundreds of millions of dollars of income. The strategy we created was to show that Roseanne had a history of denying that anyone in her life had ever really helped her—that she accomplished everything good in her life on her own, without anyone's help. For example, she had a deep bond with a sister who had helped her enormously in her career, so much so that Roseanne even dedicated a book to her. But once Roseanne reached an even higher level of fame, she eliminated her sister from her life and claimed that her sister played no role in creating her own success.

We created a column item stating that history is repeating itself—once again, Roseanne was trying to rewrite history, and turn on the very people who had propelled her to new heights of stardom. We got the story into the media, which accomplished several goals: it annoyed Roseanne, it made our case well, and it used her own words against her. Once again, you often have to win a case in the court of public opinion before you can win it in a court of law.

Oppress agentry isn't just for the wealthy, famous, and powerful. Sometimes the little guy can benefit from it as well. New York power attorney Marc Wolinsky once referred to me his client, a haircutter who worked in a leading Manhattan chain. This individual was an observant Jew. The company would not permit him to wear his yarmulke or skullcap at the salon, nor would it permit him to observe the Jewish Sabbath. We got a piece in *New York* magazine's highly influential Intelligencer column, but that only got the salon angrier at this young man, who ironically had left Eastern Europe and come to the United States in search of religious freedom.

Because *New York* magazine wasn't getting the job done, we thought we'd take it to the next level. A Fox News TV crew appeared in front of the salon and did a story on this immigrant's unhappy work experience and religious challenges. The salon buckled and offered a settlement the very next day. There's a happy ending to this story—the haircutter in question now owns his own salon. But just don't try to get your hair cut there on a Saturday.

The key to oppress agentry: sometimes you have to come out swinging. But when you do, you can't let your opponent off the mat.

There you have it: press agentry, suppress agentry, and oppress agentry—getting things into the news, keeping things out of the news, and going after somebody who's going after you. What other lessons can we learn from Hollywood? Let's find out.

CHAPTER 16

WHAT ANGELINA JOLIE KNOWS THAT YOU DON'T: COMMUNICATIONS SECRETS OF THE STARS

Not everything that comes out of Hollywood is perfect. Our industry has been known to produce a bad movie or an awful sitcom and even put together a crummy reality show.

But the reality about Hollywood is that it is one of the most successful American industries and it defines pop culture for the world. Additionally, the industry has many lessons to offer the rest of us about how to construct a successful public image. As I said earlier, the most impressive stars to me are those who cook their careers, reputations, and images in a Crock-Pot, not in a microwave. They're here today, here tomorrow, and you usually don't hear any gossip, scandal, or dirt about them. That's the kind of image-crafting that we want to talk about in this chapter. Piano legend Van Cliburn was asked what it was like to be a success after winning the prestigious Tchaikovsky competition, having a 100,000-person ticker-tape parade in his honor; and being on the cover of *Time* magazine. Only age twenty-three, he wisely answered, "I'm not a success; I'm a sensation."

Let's start with the concept of credits. Hollywood may not have invented the concept of taking credit, but it certainly has taken that concept to a new level. What do you see after every movie or TV show? All the names of all the people involved. Did you know that credits are negotiated? How big your name appears, where it is on the list, and what your title is, as in "Special Guest Star"—these are all subject to negotiation. When people realize their credits have been omitted from the movie, either before the picture or after, which is known as the "crawl," they sue. Who gets credit in Hollywood? Anyone who lifted a finger in any way to make the movie or TV show happen. This includes the caterer, the personal assistants, and even the trainees working on the film; all see their name on the screen. How important are credits? For some of the most popular Web sites on the Internet, like IMDB.com, keeping track of people's credits is part of their job.

What's the message of all this? Moviegoers end up knowing the names of actors, and often directors, producers, and screenwriters, better than we know the cashiers at the local Wal-Mart. If you're running a business that depends on good customer relations, this isn't a good thing. If you run even a small business, with customers coming in weekly, your employees ought to wear name tags, so that they are not simply faceless entities—they are real, live human beings with names and identities. And you can't assume that your customers will know, or even remember, your employees' names. Giving credit where credit is due isn't just a cliché—it's a wise business practice. Making people feel that they are part of a team definitely increases a sense of esprit de corps. You can feel that same energy in a movie studio, and you should also be able to feel it every time you walk into a business. If I were running that environmentally minded dry cleaning business, all the employees would wear nice polo shirts (green, of course), stitched with the name of the company, Clean Green Cleaners, and they'd have their name on a badge, or on their shirts as well.

It's important to identify the people who are doing the work. It actually makes them feel more special, and it helps your customers understand exactly who is there to assist them. I hate "Hello, My Name Is" stickers, so when I put together parties, I sometimes give staff members and hosts little flowers to wear on their lapels. That way, we can tell the guests, "Anybody with a red rose can help you." Everybody feels better when they know who they're dealing with and who they can approach with any question. It creates a closer and more intimate environment for all concerned. So take a lesson from Hollywood and give everybody credit for who they are and what they do. It always comes back to you.

I get a lot of credit for the things the people in my company do—getting my clients or me on TV, getting covers of magazines, whatever the case may be. I really should get credit only for hiring, mentoring, and trusting the people on my team. So I tell them, "I know I got credit for this magazine cover/interview/best-selling book, but I want you to know that you're responsible for making this happen." That's something that we all should do with our team members and especially with our employees. (To all my employees, past and present, thank you. . . . I couldn't have done it without you.) Smart stars write thank-you notes to people and build bridges, not walls. Libby Maynard, a candidate for public office for whom I worked right after college, used to write dozens of them every day, building a loyal cadre of believers who wanted her to serve.

While we're talking about appearance, one of the most important things that people in Hollywood do is that they dress for the job they want, not the job they have. If you're a Navy Seal, I'm not telling you to hit the beaches dressed like the secretary of the Navy. But part of the image you create for yourself is based on the statement your clothing makes; you never know when your "day job" will cross paths with your dreams, which is what happened for a young actor who had just done a guest part on *Frasier*. He was one of the waiters that my caterer had hired for a party at my home. David Lee, the producer of *Frasier*, was a guest, and the young actor was aghast.

"I'm kind of humiliated," the actor said, when he saw the *Frasier* producer walking through the door. "I was just on his show, and now he's going to see me doing this."

"I've known David a long time," I assured him. "I promise you he knows how much he paid you and he knows what it's like to struggle in this town, and there's nobody in this town who won't respect what you're doing." When Lee saw the actor in his waiter's uniform, he strolled over and gave him a hug. "It's great to see you," he exclaimed. "You were awesome last week. I hope we can work together again soon." That made the actor feel like a million bucks.

Stars understand that there exists no demarcation between their public and private lives. They know that they are being judged, and even photographed or videoed, every time they step into the street. If they look like hell, it's actually news. This doesn't mean that to emulate Hollywood stars you need to go into hair and makeup just to walk down to your mailbox. It is important, though, to look credible, presentable, clean, and appropriate whenever you go into any "public" forum. Remember, anyplace you might run into someone who knows you is a public forum. People are judging you not just by what you say but by how you appear. It's not shallow. It's human nature.

A number of years ago, I lost a lot of weight and I ended up hating all of my clothes. So I brought in a stylist to assist me, not for a particular red carpet event, but just to give me some perspective so that my clothing would be ready for my new life. If you were ever overweight, you probably still see that fat kid staring back at you whenever you look in the mirror, no matter how svelte you may now appear. I was the same way, and I honestly didn't have a sense of how my clothes looked on me. It's not just vanity—I can hear you snickering, but it's not. I have to present a credible public image just as much as my stars do. The stylist and I divided my wardrobe into four piles: clothing that was fine and could go back in the closet; stuff that was no good for anyone and could only be torn apart for rags; clothing that was still fine but not quite right for me and therefore to be donated; and clothing that I could alter. And then, of course, I did a little bit of shopping. As a result, I now had a look that matched the expectations of a job in the public eye like mine.

If you think that's obsessive, consider this: whenever a major celebrity, from Madonna to Larry King to Katie Couric, goes on TV, someone on their staff takes a photo of them to ensure they never wear the same outfit on television twice. When it comes to fashion, men certainly have it easier. A man can wear the same sport jacket with a different shirt underneath it a hundred times and no one will say boo. A man can wear the same tuxedo for five years if it still fits. He can dress it up with different shirts and ties as styles change, but he isn't committing a fashion faux pas. If a woman wears the same dress to two different events, she'll invariably be called on it. In Hollywood, some of the stars get to wear—and keep—clothing for specific events. In the real world, where people operate on a clothing budget, it's not possible to have a closet with two thousand suits, as former football star Deion Sanders has been reported to possess. In the real world, the key is getting a few great jackets and then accessorizing them with a different shirt, a scarf or tie, and jewelry each time. Nobody's expecting you to have a clothes budget the size of the GNP of Bolivia. Just make sure that you look appropriate each time, and wear what you wear differently enough so that you create a slightly new impression each time.

Perhaps 5 percent of Americans can figure out an appropriate wardrobe on their own. For the rest of us, it's not about hiring a stylist. It is about bringing in a trusted friend with a good eye for clothes and appearance, because it's often the case that others see us more clearly and accurately than we do. My advice is that if you were going to decorate a room in your house, you should go to the furniture store with those pictures. Same thing with fashion and looks. Consider people in the public eye—elected officials, movie stars—and ask yourself, Who looks good? Who dresses well? Whose clothing looks good, considering their weight? Who dresses in an age-appropriate manner? Sam Champion can wear things that Al Roker can't.

But there's a lot more to being successful than looking good, even in Hollywood. As I often advise young actors, you have to be prepared, be early, be professional, and be polite. It's better to be thirty minutes early than five minutes late. Listen, and don't boss the boss. For now, take direction. You don't want to get a reputation as somebody who's hard to work with, no matter how talented you are. At some point, people are going to say it's just not worth the trouble to hire you, and you don't want that. A couple of very talented people I represented at times in their careers were exquisitely talented but had miserable careers because everyone in the industry knew they were too big a pain in the ass to deal with. Life is too short.

Can you ever break the rules? My attitude is that you've got to earn the right to do so. A number of years ago, I was in the audience of *Saturday Night Live* to watch a client on the show, and I got to see Ricky Martin perform. Now, the general advice that media trainers give actors, actresses, singers, or anyone who is going to appear on television is to play to the audience, not to the camera. Let the camera follow you around. Ricky Martin ignored that advice and played directly to the camera. And it worked for him. He had been performing so long and at such a high level that he could pull it off. I met him back when he was still part of Menudo, more than twenty-five years ago. The message is that you've got to be really good to break the rules.

Similarly, Angelina Jolie did something truly remarkable when she was doing a taped interview. A reporter asked her a question she hadn't heard before, and instead of answering it immediately, she put her head down so low that it was actually out of the shot. The cameraman had nothing to shoot. Angelina collected her thoughts, then she looked at the reporter and gave a great answer. Most people couldn't get away with something like this—or could they? When we're being interviewed, sometimes we feel like a speed racer—we've got to get the right answers out in six seconds or less. Unless we're being interviewed live, they're going to edit what we say. So perhaps we can all take a lesson from Angelina Jolie: duck out of the picture for a second, compose your response, and then sit up straight and deliver it. That's a side lesson. The key piece of learning from Hollywood here: first master painting an apple, and then you can become Picasso. Learn the rules before you start to break them.

Let's move on to another important lesson that Hollywood imparts: build a strong team around you. What constitutes a Hollywood team or entourage? There's the agent, who negotiates the deal. Many have a manager, who serves as chief of staff to the team, creating and executing the vision that the star develops. And then there's the publicist—someone like me—who imparts that vision to the media. There's an attorney who vets the deals and signs off on the contracts. Since stars don't have time to run their own errands, they have personal assistants who do everything from shopping for them to picking up their dry cleaning. They'll have stylists, hair, and makeup people. Let's say a star has a particular interest in issues or ideas and wants to inspire or share a feeling of passion about those ideas. In that case, the star will most likely have a producing partner with whom he or she makes deals happen. Often there is a person running the star's foundation to make sure that their political activism has legs. And then there's a business manager making sure that there's actually enough money in the till to pay for all of these nice people.

There are often so many people on a team, so many different roles, that when I walk into a meeting there are team members I don't know. I always treat them respectfully. I never know who holds the key to power. It could be the yoga instructor. It could be the person with whom the star is having an affair. Never make the mistake of underestimating a seemingly unimportant person in a meeting, and never assume that a silent person has nothing to say.

When I build a team, I make sure, number one, that I listen to them, or they're not worth having. Number two, I build in diversity and different points of view. Nobody needs a bunch of yes-men. And number three, I encourage dissent and make it okay to disagree. "Off with your head" hasn't worked as a management tool since the French Revolution.

One of the perks of stardom is that they can get a deal at a studio that will pay for overhead—office space on the studio lot, assistants, staff members, and the like—in exchange for first look at any projects that you create. A younger star might have a parent on the team. A husband, a wife, or partner may be on-board as well. If you watch the TV show *Entourage*, you're familiar with the fact that friends are part of the team, sometimes in a formal sense and other times just informally. There might even be a spiritual adviser—an expert on the Kabbalah or Scientology. It's the responsibility of the star to put together a good team, empower them, and then let them do their jobs.

Okay, what about your team? If you're running for city council, you need a campaign manager. You need a media marketing person in charge of your ads and direct mail. You need a business manager to run the campaign's books. If you're running a business, the role of the Hollywood agent is played by your chief sales and/or marketing officer, the individual responsible for making deals happen. Your chief of staff might be your COO or your CEO. The basic idea is that individuals rarely achieve great things without a team around them. Or, to quote Senator Joseph Lieberman as he accepted the Democratic vice presidential nomination at the Los Angeles convention in 2000, "Behind every successful man is a surprised mother-in-law."

The smartest managers call team meetings when appropriate to discuss a crisis, to introduce new team members, or simply to communicate a common vision. You just want to make sure that your entire team is on the same page.

Any flakes on your team? Get rid of them. If you find out that your chief of staff has been having drinks with your opponent's chief of staff, hear him out and then fire him. You don't need anybody undercutting you or creating drama. At the same time, always listen to people on or off your team who don't have positive things to say. It's hard for us to know everything that's going on in our business or even in our lives. When someone points out something to me that I'm doing wrong or how my business can improve, I'll always say, or I try to say, "Thank you—I never would have seen it. We need to address it, and I'll fix it." All too often we become defensive when people offer criticism, whether constructive or otherwise. As an example, the owner of a local deli decided to expand into owning a nightclub. I attended a private party in his restaurant space, and it was an embarrassment. The room was dirty and they even ran out of food. Don't do that in Hollywood (or anywhere else). So I made it my business to approach him and say, "You need to know this. Here's what happened last night. Here's what I saw."

He immediately became defensive. "Are you sure you saw that?" he asked. "We're not responsible for how the room looks." And so on. He just didn't want to hear what I had to say. Unless someone is a constant complainer, hear the person out. Obviously there's a line between someone offering you a valuable perspective and someone making fun of you, as in, "You really look fat in that skirt" versus, "I think you'd look better in a darker color." There are different ways to deliver the news, and there are different motives for sharing criticism. Try to find people who are on your side before they get on your case.

Let's turn now to one of Hollywood's favorite subjects: money. You might see on *Entertainment Tonight* that a particular star just received $10 million to be in a new movie. That sounds like a lot of money, doesn't it? Let's see where the money really goes. The agent takes the first 10 percent. The manager takes the next 10 to 15 percent. The lawyer is in for 5 percent. The publicist gets a monthly fee, and the personal assistant, stylist, and hair and makeup people eat up another 5 percent. Put the business manager down for 5 percent, and in most cases, half of that $10 million has walked out the door before the star has seen a dime of it. So that $10 million suddenly becomes $5 million. This is when Uncle Sam steps in, and that $5 million gets sliced in half to $2.5 million. Tragically, stars are forced to shuffle by on $2.5 million to make a movie. Obviously, you'll never see Brad Pitt throwing a charity ball to help George Clooney make ends meet, but sometimes there is less money available at the end of the day than people might think.

The same thing is true, on a smaller scale, in television. Let's say a young actor nabs a role on a twenty-four-episode sitcom at a pay rate of $40,000 per episode. That's close to a million dollars a year. It sounds like a fortune . . . and it is. But not all of it ends up in the actor's pocket. The same team members are standing there, hats in hand: the agent, the manager, the lawyer, the publicist, the hair and makeup people, and so on down the line. That million quickly gets whittled down to $450,000 worth of pretax income, of which the government happily takes half. Okay, at $200,000 a year, you're not exactly poking around trash cans at midnight to make your next meal. But remember, if you want to go to an event, you can't wear that same dress again. You've got to go out and shop, and in Hollywood, that ain't cheap.

The media loves to embellish the biggest numbers—you never hear about a movie's net, only how much it grosses. You might hear that a film made $100 million in domestic box office receipts, but that's not too impressive if the movie cost $200 million to make and promote. What's the point? One of the most important things that Hollywood stars, top athletes, and anyone who receives windfall-style paydays have to deal with is that the money has to last a long time. Even stars have to be realistic about their spending levels. We all know Patrick Ewing's infamous quote when he played for the New York Knicks: "We make a lot, but we spend a lot, too." The late Evil Knievel had a great line about how his life had ended in bankruptcy: "I made $60 million, but I spent $61 million." Whether you're Brad Pitt or John Doe, don't live extravagantly in the eye of the public. It will hurt your image and people will not take you seriously. This is not an excuse to self-pauperize, either. The top stars look smart, efficient, and classy without being over the top. You should too.

Public relations never has the highest margins in the entertainment industry. So when I choose office space, I look for attractive, respectable workplaces, but no marble floors or outrageously expensive furniture. I don't want people saying, "That guy's got nothing but money," or worse, "That guy's got more money than taste." Don't take the penthouse for your campaign or business, but conversely, don't take your neighbor's garage as your office space, either. Show people that the way you spend money demonstrates your intelligence, concern, and thoughtfulness. No matter what you may see or hear of Hollywood excesses, the industry is committed to sensible spending. Sometimes the sensible thing is to spend a lot. But by and large, people are extremely cost conscious, and they're happiest when they're spending money that belongs to someone other than themselves. When you do spend other people's money, spend like it's your own.

We've talked about your look, we've talked about creating and empowering a great team, and we've talked about sensible spending. The next thing to remember is that what we do in our hometowns might not be international news, but if you do something silly, *your* whole world is watching. Go out with a friend from work or the boss and have a little too much wine? No problem. Grab a cab and pick your car up in the morning. But if you get out of hand at the office party and start groping the file clerks, you can expect to see that on YouTube the next morning while you're still nursing your hangover. You can also expect to be looking for a new job the next day. The Hollywood lesson: conduct yourself like a smart movie star at all times; act as if you're being watched, and even surreptitiously videoed. I'm not advocating paranoia. I'm just asking you to recognize the same thing the stars do—that the line between public and private is vanishing, not just for them, but for all of us.

We've also got to consider the company in which we are seen. We are judged by the choices we make, personally and professionally. Exactly who and what are we allowing into our lives? My first assignment after I moved to Los Angeles was for Philip Morris, the cigarette manufacturer. The Great American Smokeout had become an important event on the calendar across the country. This event, sponsored by the American Cancer Society and similar organizations nationwide, tries to persuade everybody to give up smoking for just one day. Believe me, in the corporate offices at Philip Morris, the Great American Smokeout was not exactly Christmas morning. So they came up with a concept called "The Great American Smoker." The idea was to support smokers' rights, which are dwindling, of course, in our society. As a publicist, I've worked on campaigns supporting smokers' rights, the alcohol industry, and the First Amendment aspects of the adult entertainment industry. My attitude is that if you don't know that cigarettes are bad for you, you ought to read more. Hey, so are Krispy Kreme doughnuts, but I don't see any No Doughnut days on the calendar.

I believe in personal choice and personal responsibility. Would I support a character smoking on a kids' show? Of course not. But if material is aimed at adults, I've got no problem with it. For "The Great American Smoker" campaign, Philip Morris brought the legendary comedian and cigar smoker Milton Berle onboard. His message: If you want to light up, that's fine, but let's all lighten up. Some people smoke, some don't. If you don't smoke, don't start now. But let's all respect the rights of others. This was a tasteful way to get the message out. The reason I bring it up is because we are all going to affect our public image based on the individuals, organizations, and ideas with which we align ourselves. Since I believe in personal responsibility, I have no problem working for a cigarette manufacturer. If I had a young person in my office philosophically opposed to it, I wouldn't make that person work on the account, nor would I hold it against that employee. But you've got to consider what you want to be associated with; if a choice you make isn't consistent with your public image, your public image is going to change.

An attorney can be defined by the cases he takes on, and the city council member by her voting record. If a self-avowed environmentalist lives in a 20,000-square-foot mansion with an overly watered lawn, people are going to call that person to task on it. My message: Own your decisions, because they will become an important part of the public record about you. Be prepared to explain your choices. In short, decide what your brand will be, and monitor your choices accordingly.

No matter what choices you make, you will be subject to the new way in which the news media, not just in Hollywood but across the country and most likely across the world, views celebrities national and local. We live in a "reality TV" era when it comes to celebrity news coverage. In other words, the news media depicts celebrities as if they were their own reality TV shows. Consider the way the media follows the antics of Lindsay Lohan, Britney Spears, and Paris Hilton, young women who have come to the nation's attention in part because of their ability to perform (and you can interpret that any way you like) and in part because their lives are such train wrecks. No one could create reality shows as outrageous as the lives of these three. Coverage of these individuals and others like them have created reality culture that actually translates to the way even local news covers stories.

It doesn't mean that you may or may not be voted off the island. It does mean that if you are a local public figure and you get picked up for a drunk driving offense, don't expect the local media to give you a pass, as it might have a decade or so ago. Bad news is hard news, and celebrity bad news is the hardest news of all. They used to say, "If it bleeds, it leads," meaning that on local news, a violent accident or gruesome crime would always be the first story of the day. Today, it's not so much about what's gruesome as about what's shocking and tawdry. That's what glues eyeballs to the screen. So if you are a conspicuous or public person, no matter how big or small your fishbowl, remember that everything you do and say can and will be used against you.

When should you become media conscious? The moment that you decide that you're going to set a new goal for yourself—the day you reach the conclusion that you want to attain something more. You don't want to wait until your campaign comes out to be aware of what the media will say about you. A friend of mine was the president of marketing for one of the studios. He told me, "The PR campaign for a film starts with the moment I announce it. It doesn't begin when the ads appear, or when I release the trailers. It begins the moment I say anything at all about the film."

The first time he says something about a studio project is when there's big news. His first announcement might be about an A-level director and two A-level stars who have been green-lighted for a film with an $80 million budget, an epic that will take ten weeks to shoot in Uruguay. That's the way you announce something important—with big news. You don't start off and say the second leading role in a new film has been given to a particular character actor who seems to be in just about every movie ever made. Make it big from the start.

What happens when you follow the recipe in this book and you do have stardom in your world? In that case, take a lesson from the actors and actresses with the "Crock-Pot careers," not the microwave variety who will be here and gone in sixty seconds. I'm talking about people like Jack Nicholson, Cameron Diaz, Brad Pitt, George Clooney, and Julia Roberts. You rarely see a negative word about them. They have their difficulties, like everyone else, but their challenge is no longer to get in the public eye. Any A-level star can get any interview, any magazine cover, with the snap of his or her fingers. They can also dictate the terms of a photo shoot—where it will be, when it will be, and what photographer will be involved. Their issue now is managing and controlling the press. So once your public image develops critical mass, the trick is to remain in the public eye by continuing to do newsworthy things . . . and letting people know that you're doing them. Again, doing the work is only half the battle. The other half is letting the world know what you've done.

It's not all a bed of roses. The downside is that you are in the public eye, and as we've discussed earlier, the distinction between the public and private is diminishing at a frightening rate. In Hollywood, you'll be stared at. People will actually steal your trash. You could be stalked. They'll know where you live. They'll know where you are at any time, thanks to the notorious Gawker Stalker, which we talked about earlier. Rebecca Schaeffer and John Lennon are among celebrities who ended up dead because of fans' obsessions. The fan who killed Rebecca Schaeffer was able to get her address by paying one dollar to the California Department of Motor Vehicles. That law has changed, but it's still easy to find people, all too easy. Tennis legend Martina Navratilova told me that she's okay when a normal person comes up to her at a normal time asking for an autograph, but sometimes people will just come up, touch her, and shout out, "I just touched a famous person!" Is that what you want to go through?

Wear the same dress twice and they'll make fun of you. Party too hard, and you'll see yourself the next morning—or even that same night—on TMZ.com. If you yell at your kid, the baby-sitter might sell the tape. Or if you're sleeping with the baby-sitter, she might sell that one too. When we went through the Paris Hilton jail saga, L.A. looked like Baghdad, with television trucks speeding everywhere and helicopters darkening the skies overhead. If you're famous, it's not like you're reclining on some sort of pasha-mobile, carried around town by four strapping, shirtless men. Celebrities have to go to the drugstore for rash ointment just like everyone else. The only problem is that their rash suddenly becomes international news. As Liz Taylor put it, as we were in a freight elevator heading to an event, "The bigger the star, the worse the elevator."

Not everybody ends up as fodder for the celebrity gossip machine. Consider Meryl Streep. She lives quietly in the country, doesn't attend many Hollywood parties, goes to work, picks up her Oscars, and goes home. She enjoys recognition as one of the finest actors (the preferred Hollywood term for actors *and* actresses) of our time. So there's a distinction between recognition and fame. Meryl Streep is recognized for her great talent. Paris Hilton is merely famous for being famous.

Another thing that's fun to do is to bring Hollywood to your hometown. We've already talked about how to bring celebrities in. What do you do once you have them there? Or what do you do with people in your community to make them feel like celebrities? Have a red carpet. There must be one lying around somewhere. Hire a bunch of college kids to take photos and assume the position of paparazzi. Nothing makes people feel more like stars than having their picture taken again and again and again. Give out gift bags—everybody loves free stuff. And have a banner with logos of your event's sponsors at some point along the red carpet, so that photographers can take pictures with your stars standing in front of the banner.

If you get sponsors for your event, the way you pay them back is by placing multiple small versions of their logo on a banner, which, thanks to the Internet, school kids could produce on their computers. We call it a "step and repeat." Why do you want a lot of little logos instead of a few big ones? Because it's all too easy for somebody to stand in front of a letter or word, and suddenly your sponsor's logo is blocked. Who's a good sponsor? Moët & Chandon Champagne and Ford Motor Company are the kinds of companies that sponsor events in Hollywood. If I were putting on an event in another city, I might turn to the leading liquor store and ask that business to donate wine to the event in exchange for sponsorship privileges. Instead of Ford Motor Company, I would go to the local dealership and invite them to place their logo on the banner in exchange for financial support. If you go this route, don't expect a sign and banner company to give you a free banner. After all, that's their business. But it never hurts to ask for a charity or not-for-profit rate. That benefits you and them—just make sure there's a legitimate reason for a given sponsor to come onboard. If you've got an environmental event, Exxon may not be your first choice. But the green cleaners would be a perfect sponsor.

As I've already mentioned, in 2007–2008, a writers' strike shut down production in Hollywood. When I drove by the writers' picket lines in front of the movie and television studios, it reminded me of my childhood, when I would occasionally see General Motors workers out on strike. The mornings were cold, and the striking workers would be trying to keep themselves warm by burning wood scraps in barrels on the picket lines. Contrast that image with striking writers enjoying scones passed out on silver trays by representatives of talent agencies. That's not exactly the way to win the PR war.

The writers would have been much better advised to make clear, not just to Hollywood insiders but to all Americans, that their struggle is the same as everyone else's—to maintain the middle class in the face of corporate greed. In 2006, Writers Guild members earned $60 million in DVD residuals, one of the key battlegrounds in the strike. Also in 2006, one Viacom executive received a $60 million buy-out package—so one executive took home the same amount of money as did all of the writers that whole year. Why didn't the writers make more use of that fact? The lesson: If you're in a war, take your best shot. Make your story relevant to the broadest number of people in your world. Manage your image, and don't let anybody feed scones on silver trays to your striking workers.

Even famous, experienced actors sometimes get it wrong. My friend *L.A. Times* reporter Jeanine Stein was assigned to cover the premiere of a film starring Billy Crystal. She went up to him at the party afterward and he told her he was tired and "done for the night." She wrote a very impassioned and intelligent column explaining that she was tired too, but they both had jobs to do. It became the talk of the town.

Finally, while it sounds morbid, Hollywood even offers guidance on the best way to die. Celebrities die just as do normal people, perhaps with a little flourish, but they die just the same. In Hollywood, death is a chance to define oneself for posterity. It reminds me of the line from the beginning of Neil Simon's play *The Sunshine Boys*; two old vaudevillians are commenting on the recent passing of a fellow performer:

"Where'd he die?" one asked.

"In *Variety*," his friend responded.

Even death can be spun. I worked with the great actress Elizabeth Montgomery. She didn't really like the media and did little press. She discovered that she had terminal cancer, and she wanted to make sure that her death would be treated in a digni-fied manner. In our last conversation, she thanked me for every-thing I had done for her over the years, and then she looked me in the eye and said, "And don't forget, Howard. I'm fifty-seven years old."

She wasn't fifty-seven years old. If you want to know exactly how old she was, you'll have to look it up somewhere else. It's not exactly a state secret. She was born into a well-known acting family. Her father was the great Robert Montgomery. Everyone who cared to find out could discover quickly when she was born and how old she was.

Not long before the end, I received a call from *People* maga-zine that I consider the most offensive media call I've received in my entire career. "If Elizabeth dies by three o'clock Wednesday afternoon," the breathless *People* person told me, "we'll give her the cover."

Sarcastically I replied, "What do you want me to do, go to the hospital and smother her with a pillow?"

Obviously it was sick and inappropriate, but we can all have our bad taste moments here and there.

When Elizabeth passed, I called the media and alerted them to the fact that her age was fifty-seven.

"Howard," some of the reporters said, "she wasn't fifty-seven."

I explained that being listed as fifty-seven in the media was the last wish of a dying woman. I had some victories and some losses with that campaign, but the AP, which did the biggest story on Elizabeth Montgomery's death, said that she was fifty-seven.

You'd have thought the media had become bewitched.

CHAPTER 17

HOW TO MAKE A GREAT SPEECH, HOLLYWOOD-STYLE

The good news about being in the public eye is that you now get to make speeches about the topics, ideas, and themes that mean the most to you.

The bad news about being in the public eye is that now you *have to* make speeches about those same things. They say that most people are terrified of making speeches. How can you be comfortable enough on the podium so that people won't be terrified to listen to you?

There's actually a lot you can do to prepare yourself for those moments when you do have to get up and say a few words.

If you dislike the whole idea of speechifying, from getting up and making a toast at a wedding to standing in a ballroom before a crowd of a thousand or more, you're not alone. Ron Meyer, the chairman of Universal Studios, is a wonderful public speaker. Fifteen years ago he wasn't. He hated the idea of public speaking. At the time, he was running Creative Artists Agency, one of the world's most powerful talent agencies. He came to me for speech advice for remarks he was delivering at AIDS Project Los Angeles's legendary benefit, Commitment to Life.

"Howard, I haven't given a speech since my bar mitzvah," he told me.

The first thing I asked Ron was based on a concept with which you've become quite familiar through the previous chapters of this book—What are your messages? A good speech contains three to five messages, just the same way a PR campaign does. Ron and I started off by concentrating on what his messages would be. Once he knew the three or four things that he wanted to be sure to tell the group, we talked about anecdotes that would bolster the speech and make the points more memorable for the listeners. Humor is a wonderful ice breaker in a speech, especially when you position yourself as the butt of the joke. It humanizes you, increases empathy on the part of your listeners, and just makes everything a little more comfortable for all concerned.

Ron had his messages, and his anecdotes. If that sounds familiar, it's because that's exactly how you prepare for your radio, TV, and print interviews. This stuff is getting easier, isn't it? I hope so. It's pretty straightforward when you start thinking about it. Ron's next task was to write out his whole speech. If you do have a longer speech to give, I advocate writing out the entire speech on your computer, or dictating it and having someone transcribe it for you. Once you've written it out, read it out loud. The written word and the spoken word are two different things, and what works on the page may not work quite as well when you are reading it.

Were there any volatile buzzwords that needed to be either included or omitted? What flash points, if any, might there have been in his speech? These were the things we looked for as Ron and I went over the draft.

Is it okay to read a speech? Depending on the circumstances, it can be. If you're making an important address to a large gathering, it doesn't hurt to have a draft of the speech available to you, either on the podium with you or via teleprompter. But when you go up there, the last thing you want to do is fumble around for your speech, trying to remember what pocket to pull it out of, trying to find your glasses, and so on. We'll talk more about performance practice for actually making the speech, but for right now, if you are going to read it, print out a copy in big print so you never get lost trying to find your place.

Ideally, you won't read your speech from a script. Who do you want to be, Gerald Ford? You'll know your three to five messages, you'll know your anecdotes, and you'll have practiced it countless times. After you get over your initial nervousness about being on stage, it will flow beautifully. If you want to keep your three to five messages typed out in large print—again, I emphasize large print so that you can actually see the darned thing while you're up there—on an index card, that's fine. The best speeches come off as improvised right on the spot. It can take an awful lot of work to make it look as though you are just simply delivering off-the-cuff remarks instead of reciting a speech that you've labored over. But the more relaxed and confident you are on stage, the better things will go.

Ron's next step was to read the speech to his wife and to a few other trusted friends and associates. It makes a big difference to have other people hear the speech—they're going to pick up on things that you might not identify. They might suggest to you that you're taking a little too long to get to a point, or that perhaps a point isn't being made clearly enough. If you can't find someone to whom to read the speech, then read it to yourself in the mirror. It's hard to give ourselves accurate feedback, but it's better than not having anybody at all.

Within a few days, Ron had taken the speech to another level. He worked with it, improved the sense of flow, added a few more anecdotes, and made it authentic to himself. When he went up to actually deliver the speech, he did a great job. And today, Ron is as outstanding a speaker as you'll find in or out of Hollywood.

Contrast Ron's experience with what happens with a typical Academy Awards recipient. The person rushes up on stage, fumbles around for the reading glasses, and fumbles around for the speech, which is basically a list of names that no one's ever heard of nor could possibly care less about, written out in the limo on the way to the theater, with some champagne stains, maybe some hairspray, perhaps some makeup, making it barely legible. And *this* is how Oscar winners use their brief moment in the sun. I'm not too impressed with that.

Frankly, there's nothing more boring than that long list of names, which ends up sounding like the board of directors of a B'nai B'rith lodge. I've been lucky enough to coach a few important people making those speeches, and I can share with you some of the guidance I gave them. Steve Tisch won an Oscar for producing *Forrest Gump*. If you think back to that movie, just about everybody claimed that the movie supported their point of view. The right wing said the film was conservative because Forrest served in the military. The liberals said no, Forrest is liberal—he's nonjudgmental and he helps a woman who is having a baby out of wedlock.

Steve and I focused on a very important point—that no matter how big your movie is, there are still plenty of people who haven't seen it, and the Oscars are a great way to get people to buy your movie on DVD. Consider this: a film could gross $100 million at the domestic box office, and that's pretty substantial by practically any reckoning. This means that less than 15 million people have seen your film. But this is a country of 300-plus-million people, so there are plenty of moviegoers left who could still be influenced to see your film. Reading off that boring list of team members isn't going to get anybody to go to the movie theater or to Blockbuster or to Netflix or to buy a DVD. Even if 50 million people saw *Forrest Gump*, there are still 250 million Americans who haven't seen it, not to mention billions of people around the world. Sometimes Hollywood offers an object lesson in how not to do things. When you see those Academy Award winners going on with those interminable lists, you know that Hollywood's getting it wrong. The right thing to do? Think about your messages. It always goes back to your messages. Make any speaking engagement an opportunity to get your messages out to your world.

Steve Tisch got it right. He went up on stage and said something to the effect that "People on both sides of the political spectrum have tried to claim this film for their own. In the end, *Forrest Gump* is not about Democrats or Republicans, liberals or conservatives—it's about simple humanity." Steve hit a grand slam with those words. That was the quote picked up in boldface in the *L.A. Times* and in newspapers around the world. He got his message out, and he increased people's curiosity about seeing the movie if they hadn't already seen it. That's the right way to do it.

Whom should you thank if you win an Academy Award, or any award? Instead of the impersonal list of names, make your thank-you's personal and sincere. Let's say you're winning an Oscar for acting. Perhaps you didn't like the script when you first read it, but someone on your team told you you'd be a schmuck if you turned it down. Tell the story and thank your manager. Tilda Swinton did just that in singling out her agent, Brian Swardstrom. If you had an amazing experience working with someone on the film, say that: "I want to thank Oliver Stone because he taught me what acting is all about." How did Steve Tisch handle the personal side of his Academy Award speech? He had a great line. He said, "I want to thank my four best friends." Steve is such a likable guy that there must have been dozens of people who thought they were among the four best friends he thanked in his speech. Again, Steve got it right.

Cathy Schulman won an Oscar for producing *Crash*. At the time of that Academy Award ceremony, she was going through a very contentious situation, including lawsuits with one of the coproducers. For Cathy, going up and getting the award was her special moment. She used her time to acknowledge the fact that many independent films had been nominated that year, so she gave a nod to the other independent filmmakers. Her speech was very well received. Incidentally, Cathy and I spent a week shopping for the right dress, getting her hair and makeup right, the whole gestalt. She's a very beautiful woman, but I wanted her to look like a producer, not a movie star. You always want to appear to be what you are instead of trying to create a look inappropriate for yourself. Cathy looked so beautiful that Michael Kors, the great designer, called her the next day to tell her how hot she was and how wonderful she looked in the dress that he had designed. So if you have the privilege of accepting an award, use it as one more opportunity to reinforce your messages to the broadest possible audience.

Crash was a surprise winner and Cathy was, frankly, shocked. In her speech, she actually thanked her husband and her wife. When she came backstage in the Kodak Theater and I was waiting for her, she said, "I know I said 'my husband and my wife,' but when I said 'wife,' I meant you, Howard." It had been an intensely busy week.

Let's say you're not accepting an award—let's say that you've been given the opportunity to make a speech to an organization important to the cause you espouse, to your business, or to whatever else you are doing in order to reach the next level in your life. Before you accept the invitation, ask yourself whether there really is a good reason for making the speech. Is this a good audience for you? Is this a good opportunity for you to get your messages out? Is the timing right? If you get too many no's to these questions, gracefully decline the invitation. You're better off not speaking at all than making a speech to an inappropriate group.

The best metaphor for speeches is the wedding toast. Many of us have been called upon from time to time to get up and say a few words at a wedding. The same keys that make a wedding toast effective will make your speech before any group powerful and memorable. The first thing you want to ask yourself is whether you are the star of the show or a member of the supporting cast, and tailor your speech appropriately to your role. Are you the groom's brother and best man? Are you the father of the bride? In that case, you do want to put a certain amount of preparation into your speech, because while you are not the main star of the show, you are certainly up there.

If you're a coworker, a college friend, or a member of the

wedding party, that's terrific. But people don't really want to hear a long speech from you, do they? When I make a wedding toast, I always ask myself what makes my relationship with the bride or groom unique. What do I know about them that would offer enjoyable insight into their lives? Obviously, there is a certain obligation to be appropriate, which tends to be forgotten as the liquor flows. So you want to make sure that your message is appropriate to the gathering, and that it reflects a point of view that everyone present will find enjoyable and perhaps even instructive.

The same thing is true with any speech you make to any group. Before you go up, find out how long you are expected to speak, and don't go any longer. The last thing you want is for people to be looking at their watches as your speech drones on and on, wondering when the mushroom risotto will be served.

Another great thing to do in order to prepare for a speech is to go up to the podium before it's time for your appearance and just get a feel for the environment up there. Politicians and business leaders call this "doing advance work," which means that a staffer makes sure that the presidential seal is in the right place, that the teleprompter is at the right height, that the microphones are squared away, and so on. You can do your own advance work simply by stepping up to the podium while no one else is paying attention. If you're at a wedding and you're going to make a toast, the guests might be in the other room having hors d'oeuvres and cocktails. That's a great time for you to step up to the microphone, put your hands on the podium, check the lighting, take a look at where people are seated, and generally make yourself comfortable up there. The overall process we're discussing here is one of desensitization. You want to remove as much of the fear as possible by removing the unknown elements from your speech-making process.

You've already written out your speech, laid in your messages and anecdotes, and reduced it to bullet points on an index card or perhaps committed the whole thing to memory. Now we're trying to get you just as comfortable with the setting as with the words you will say. This way, when you get up there and nervousness strikes, your "muscle memory" will kick in—you'll remember that you've been up on this particular podium before just to check things out, and that will increase your comfort level. And you've been over your speech so often that you'll end up doing it the right way. For all the fears that people have about public speaking, the reality is that abject, embarrassing failure happens far less often than we fear. When was the last time you saw someone make a fool of himself at the podium? If you have ever seen something like that, it's almost always due to the speaker's lack of preparation, and that's not going to be your problem.

Once you're called on and you get up there to make your speech, take a moment and get settled. Take a few seconds and look around the room, get comfortable physically before you even say a word. No one will mind. You don't have to launch right in—in fact, people will be more comfortable if they see that you are. That leads to one of the most important points I can share with you: studies have shown repeatedly that what people take away from a speech has little to do with the words you speak and more with who you are and how you are at the podium. In other words, they remember you far more than they remember the speech over which you have labored for days or even weeks. As the expression goes, "Who you are speaks so loudly that I can hardly hear a word you're saying."

Use hand gestures authentically and sparingly. Don't point. That implies "you people." Bad. When you outstretch your hand for emphasis, keep your index finger bent and your thumb on top—like a nonaggressive fist.

Okay—you've written your speech, you've delivered it, you've received a thunderous ovation, and shouts of "Encore!" and "More!" are ringing in your ears. Should you give them another ten minutes? Absolutely not. One of the most important things that Hollywood teaches is to always leave your audience hungry for a little more. Let them wish they heard more of you instead of leaving them with the feeling that you went on a little too long. There may not be an orchestra swelling in the background to tell you that you are overstaying your welcome on stage, but people have a mental "hook," and before you know it, you'll have an entire room checking their e-mails or their stocks or the scores of the ballgame—anything rather than listening to you for much longer.

I know you're not going to make that mistake. (If you do, don't tell them you read my book.) Once you've come down from the podium, if you are in a situation in which you are making news, you are most likely going to be interviewed by the media. This is yet another opportunity for you to get your messages out. Once you step down from the podium and head to the media room for a news conference, you can expect more questions about that topic. Be prepared with three to five messages, and get your points out clearly and succinctly. That's the right way to do it.

One last thing: when you go up to make your speech, turn off your cell phone. It's distracting enough if someone in the audience gets a call during your speech. The last thing you want is to be standing up there trying to remember in what pocket you put your phone. Don't laugh—it happened to Rudy Giuliani while he was campaigning for president—more than once. You see where it got him.

It may sound hard to believe, but public speaking can actually become enjoyable. After all, you have messages that you want to get out to the world, and audiences are waiting to hear your message.

So prepare your speech, acclimate yourself to the speaking environment, and get up there and knock it out of the park.

CHAPTER 18

COMING OUT OF THE CLOSET, OR "I'VE GOT A SECRET"

Y ou've got a secret.

It's a piece of information about your personal life, your relationship history, your sexual orientation, or perhaps a brush with the law. Whatever it is, if people knew about it, they might look at you in a different way. And here you are, crafting a new public image. What are you supposed to do about this private matter?

This chapter is all about the difference between coming out of the closet, the term the gay world uses to describe individuals who make a choice to publicly declare their status as gay or lesbian, versus being "outed," which is the aggressive act of an individual or organization to publicly reveal the sexual orientation of an individual who might have wanted to keep it private.

If the whole question of gays and lesbians doesn't relate to you or your life, you might be wondering what all this has to do with you. I bring this in as prologue to the idea that whatever issue or skeleton might be hanging around in your closet, you've got to make the critical decision now rather than later whether you want to get ahead of the issue and bring it out into the public sphere or risk the fact that someone—a reporter or an enemy—might bring it out for you, and not at a time or in a manner of your choosing. It's ludicrous to think that a secret will be a secret for long, especially if you are entering the public eye. We've seen time and again how individuals thought that their pasts were well buried, but a simple Google search of their own names might have revealed otherwise. You can see where I'm going with all this—I'm a big believer in getting something on the table ahead of time, because you don't want to be outed for something at a time when you are trying to get your all-important messages out to the world.

The first thing to do is to recognize that in your world, just as in the world of celebrities, the line between public and private is eroding on a daily basis. What used to be nobody's business in the past is, today, something that everybody knows about or might find out.

So what do you do?

The best advice in a situation like this is to get ahead of the story, to control it so that you don't find yourself "outed." You don't want that piece of information used against you. During the 2008 presidential campaign, Senator Barack Obama addressed the issue of his early experimentation with drugs, a matter he "came out" with years earlier in his book, *Dreams from My Father*. By breaking the story, he turned the whole thing into a nonstory. Imagine if he had never brought the issue to the fore during his campaign. His opponents, performing routine opposition research, surely would have dug it up, or the media might have found it first. Either way, the story would have broken at the least opportune moment and cost him the maximum goodwill and favorable publicity. Instead of promoting his own agenda, he would be backpedaling and having to defend himself against these "charges." Frankly, I'm not sure I'm ready for America to be ruled by an individual who *hasn't* experimented with illegal drugs. I mean, who would be left to choose from? But Obama chose the wise course. He got out in front of the issue, instead of letting it fester and eventually get him into trouble.

When David Patterson became governor of New York after his predecessor resigned following a scandal, one of his first official acts was to hold a news conference. He didn't talk about his vision for the state or his legislative agenda—he admitted that he and his wife had had extramarital affairs, effectively putting the issue behind them.

My friend David Kopay, the professional football player, came out decades ago during his football career. Back then, nobody would have outed him. Nobody would have written about it, wanted to touch the story, or even believed that a pro-football player could be gay. By contrast, Pete Williams, the press secretary at the Pentagon, found himself outed—his homosexuality, which he had sought to keep to himself, was publicly reported, against his wishes, by a gay magazine that objected to his hypocritical stance with regard to gays and lesbians in the military.

We can extend the concept of coming out of the closet far beyond its original reference to gays and lesbians. Today, an individual might "come out" with regard to a prior divorce, or a possible career change, or it might be something of which we might not be so proud—a prior drunk driving conviction, a skirmish with the IRS, or experimentation with drugs. As you move into the limelight, the question is whether you want or need to get this information into the public record instead of having it lurking in your background, waiting to be discovered. In this chapter, we will discuss the concept of coming out versus running the risk of being outed, and we'll see how to make the appropriate choice.

I know what it's like to be an outsider—I grew up a fat, Jewish, gay guy in Flint, Michigan. In Hollywood, those are the first three rungs up the ladder of success, but in a town like Flint, it's three strikes and you're out. It's a little like that *Twilight Zone* episode with a whole planet full of deformed people and they make fun of the normal guy. You just have to be in the right place for you. I've been out of the closet—open about my sexual orientation—for a very long time, going all the way back to when I graduated college and began my professional life more than thirty years ago. I made the choice early on to live honestly and authentically for me.

When the time came for me to come out, I sat down with my parents, coworkers, and friends and told them the truth about myself. Back then, in the world in which I grew up, people didn't openly talk about gays and lesbians. Ours was an invisible society, not in the news, not on TV shows. Today, of course, everything has changed. Kids come home from school and instead of watching *Leave It to Beaver*, they're watching *Queer Eye for the Straight Guy* or *Will and Grace*. Today, tabloids and Web sites openly speculate about the sexual orientation of various celebrities. The *National Enquirer* actually runs a feature naming who's gay and who's not. It's hard for celebrities to control this aspect of their lives, particularly if they have a partner and are not seen dating members of the opposite sex. Back in the day, the homosexuality of a star like Rock Hudson was an open secret in Hollywood, but the media wouldn't write about it. As we've discussed, in the old days, the media and the movie studios were in cahoots to keep the images of stars protected, in order to protect the almighty box office. Now, in the era of citizen journalism, the media finds itself in a mad rush to get information out, without any regard for how much it might hurt a given person.

The whole question of outing people places the media, both mainstream and gay, in a conundrum. It's not as though people come out or get outed all the time. Perhaps only one or two celebrities a year either make this decision (or have it made for them). In today's world, that number might be accelerating to the point where there might be three or four big names, but it does not occur dozens of times. The media still isn't exactly sure how to deal with all this.

Liz Smith once wrote an item in her column about two Hollywood executives who were dating and split up because one of them was dating a third. In this story, all three of the individuals were men, and Liz Smith, intentionally or inadvertently, outed all three before coming out herself years later. Was it a shock to the gay community in Hollywood to read about these three men? Well, we didn't exactly drop our mint juleps. In her mind, whether one was straight or gay was no big deal. The juicy part of the story was the love triangle. If this is mainstream acceptance, I guess we'll have to take it.

In that case, the three men did not know that they were going to be written up in Liz Smith's nationally syndicated column. But twenty years ago, Arthur Ashe knew that *U.S.A. Today* was going to run with the story that he was infected with the HIV virus, a fact that he had tried to keep confidential. He was forced to have a press conference in which he acknowledged that he did indeed have the HIV virus. More recently, CIA agent Valerie Plame was outed by enemies in power. Whether it has to do with one's sexuality or one's career, outing is indeed an aggressive act. And it doesn't just happen to gays and spies. A celebrity who is getting married, a celebrity who is pregnant, a celebrity who goes to rehab, or a celebrity who leaves rehab early might find himself or herself on TMZ.com or somewhere else on the Internet.

Which begs this question: with the wall between public and private collapsing, why do celebrities even bother trying to keep things private? Well, sometimes people have a good reason to keep something out of the news. A star who discovers that she is pregnant may wish to keep that information out of the public prints because she might have gone through two or three miscarriages or unsuccessful pregnancies in the past, and she doesn't want to say anything until she knows this time it's for real. Or a person might receive bad news about cancer and hasn't yet had the opportunity to tell his parents. In cases like these, the media has no business outing someone. And yet, sometimes things happen by mistake. Tom Hanks inadvertently outed his high school drama teacher when accepting an Oscar for his role as a gay man in the movie *Philadelphia*. That event triggered the development of the Kevin Kline movie *In and Out*. Tom Hanks was not acting maliciously. Indeed, when it comes to HIV/AIDS and other gay-related issues, Tom Hanks has always been one of the good guys. Sometimes, things come out just by mistake.

I've developed a reputation in Hollywood as the go-to guy

for stars who decide to come out. The first celebrities I took out of the closet were Dick Sargent, Darren number two on *Bewitched*, and Sheila Kuehl, now an elected official in California and initially an actor on the 1960s TV sitcom *The Loves and Lives of Dobie Gillis*. Ironically, on a personal note, when I was thirteen, I came with my family to California for a cousin's wedding. Somehow my parents and I got in to see the filming of *Bewitched*, which was filmed without a live audience. It was just shot in a studio. The only Hollywood stars I met on that trip were Elizabeth Montgomery, Dick Sargent, and Agnes Moorehead. Of those three, I ended up working with two of them, Montgomery and Sargent. Elizabeth always believed that *Bewitched* was the perfect metaphor for being in the closet. Anytime Samantha used her powers as a witch, she had to close the doors, pull the drapes, and make sure that no one could see what was happening. Today, Samantha might be able to come out of the closet herself and practice her witchcraft for all to see, but that's not how things were back then.

When Dick Sargent decided to come out, I called *Entertainment Tonight* to get an interview for him. He laughed at the thought—he hadn't been on TV for decades, and he couldn't believe that anyone would care. Yet by coming out of the closet, he got thousands of fan letters from viewers gay and straight, who basically said, "God bless you for living your life honestly." Then he started getting additional roles from casting directors who hadn't given him a second thought in years. Typically, when actors come out, good things happen.

Along the same lines, Tom Villard's claim to fame consisted of roles in sitcoms in the 1980s, but ten years later, he developed AIDS and was on the verge of losing his Screen Actors Guild health insurance. He decided to come out of the closet hoping that someone might hire him and give him enough days to allow him to keep his health insurance. A wonderful casting lady, indeed one of the preeminent individuals in the field of casting, became the unsung hero in the story. Mary Jo Slater immediately called and found a part for this actor. You might be familiar with

Mary Jo's son, Christian Slater. To me, she's a hero. She never asked for praise—she did it because it was the right thing to do.

I've also worked with a number of actors right after they came out. Mitchell Anderson of *Doogie Howser* and *Party of Five* came out on the spur of the moment at a benefit dinner. He called me the next day to ask, "What the hell did I just do?" Amanda Bearse, famous for her role on *Married with Children*, came out as a lesbian and I helped her as well. Ironically, when Amanda, Mitchell, or any individual, comes out, the media immediately views that person as an expert on everything to do with gay rights, from legal rights for gays in Hawaii to AIDS, from current events to legal decisions, from medical issues related to HIV to just about anything under the sun. Not everyone wants to get involved politically, and just because you come out doesn't mean you've got all the background in the world at your fingertips. My attitude is, give people a chance to find their way.

A perfect example of this is the story of Esera Tuaolo, an NFL player who decided to come out. He had no book or TV show to promote. He simply wanted to come out in order to "live in his truth." He had a partner and they had adopted children. He wanted to be able to walk around town proudly with his partner at his side, his head held high. When you have a national figure to take out of the closet, the first story is very, very important. You don't want a press conference and a media frenzy. I'm a big believer in controlling the release of a story as sensitive as this. Bob Lipsyte, the legendary *New York Times* sportswriter, did a piece that demonstrated his incredible sensitivity toward this issue. *Real Sports with Bryant Gumbel* on HBO came up next and did a very fine story as well, and then Tuaolo appeared on *Good Morning America*, whose studios overlook Times Square. The show was broadcasted live on a JumboTron screen in Times Square, and when Tuaolo emerged from the studio, he came out as a hero. Real New Yorkers—the hot dog vendors and cops on the street, no quiche eaters they—hailed Tuaolo as a star and a hero for his courage. They were giving him free hot dogs, free T-shirts—you would never have believed it was New York.

Do gays in Hollywood have an entirely smooth path at this point? Of course not. It's okay for Tom Hanks to play a gay guy, but openly gay actors still have trouble getting roles as straight men. I find this double standard silly. It might be in its final days, though. Neil Patrick Harris, of the TV shows *How I Met Your Mother* and *Doogie Howser*, came out, as did T. R. Knight of *Grey's Anatomy*. The stigma is disappearing now that gay actors are playing straight people credibly and openly.

Early in my career I had an experience with a straight actor who was shy about his heterosexuality. The talented and charming Doug Savant, who is a big star on *Desperate Housewives*, started his career by playing a gay man on *Melrose Place*. As Doug's publicist, people were always asking about his personal sexual orientation. He is in fact heterosexual, married, and has numerous children. But Doug thought it would be insulting to the gay community if he went out of his way to say he was straight so we kept his embarrassing heterosexuality in the closet for a long time. One of the most decent guys in town, Doug didn't even fire me when I broke his ankle at a charity event. I'll save that story for the talk show circuit.

The openness in today's world extends from the world of entertainment into the worlds of sports and commerce. Olivia .com is the largest travel company specializing in meeting the needs of the lesbian community. Olivia hired Rosie Jones, one of the ten most successful female golfers of all time, as its public face. Olivia wanted to take her out of the closet when they announced her sponsorship. While Esera Tuaolo had a wonderful exuberance about coming out because he wanted to be a political activist, Rosie Jones, by contrast, didn't want to be a poster child for anything. She just wanted to come out. That's what I call equality—when a person can just be herself and himself, without a media expectation that he or she will play an important role in public discourse.

Evidence of this new era can be found from the AARP's choice of Martina Navratilova as its health and fitness spokesperson. They chose her not because of the gay/straight issue. They chose her because she is the best example of an individual remaining fit into her fifties and that's what they wanted to depict.

The gay community itself doesn't always make it easy for those who come out. Sheryl Swoopes, the great WNBA star, was the first pro-athlete to come out at the peak of her career since Olympic swimming medalist Greg Louganis. When I met Sheryl, she was quite upset because she was facing enormous disapproval from the power brokers in the lesbian community. Sheryl wasn't buying the party line, and was telling the world that her decision to become a lesbian was a choice. She had been married to a man, and that experience wasn't satisfying, and therefore she had made this decision. That's not the image the community wanted to project about itself. Sheryl told me, "I know I'm supposed to say what they want me to say, but that's not my truth." I told her that she had the right to tell her story without shaping it to the popular political will. The gay/lesbian community was not happy. Swoopes received tremendous press. She was everywhere. But I think that's a measure of freedom—it's important to be able to come out on your own terms and not terms dictated by the powers-that-be in the gay and lesbian community.

I've already recounted the story of NBA player John Amaechi, who called me in late 2006 because he had heard that I was the idiot savant of taking athletes out of the closet. And as we've seen, Amaechi's revelations received massive attention both in the sports and entertainment media. He prepared the ground for his coming out in an effective way, and the world embraced him for doing so.

So if you are going to come out about anything, what's the right way to do it? First, tell your family, your loved ones, and the people with whom you work. Don't let them be caught by surprise. You don't want them to read it in the newspaper, when you should have told them directly. Think about your target audiences and think about the best ways to bring the news to them in a sensitive and acceptable manner. And also keep in mind that you may have to come out again and again. In the case of Dave Kopay, the former NFL player, people simply forgot that he was gay, and he did have to remind people on repeated occasions of his orientation. And if the issue over which you are coming out is politically charged, have your media responses prepared ahead of time. A few years back, the governor of New Jersey was in a love triangle—he was a married man. When he resigned, he claimed the banner of being a "gay American," as if that were some sort of hyphenate, like being a Polish-American or a Cuban-American. Please. It wasn't well thought out and felt inauthentic.

The bottom line: the history that I've shared with you in this chapter about gays and lesbians coming out of the closet can serve as a metaphor for you and the secrets in your life. What do you want the world to know about you? What might you rather hold back, and what is the likelihood that if you do enter the public eye, someone or some entity will bring this information out about you? With whom should you share this information before you go public? What's the best way for you to control the story? Is there a journalist with whom you have a good relationship, who is likely to give you and your issue a fair hearing? Would it be more appropriate to put something on your Web site, or on a MySpace page?

Keep in mind that practically everyone who has stepped forward and admitted an uncomfortable truth ended up being in a better place, personally and professionally. I can't think of a person who came out and was less happy or was displeased with the results, because truth is so powerful. If we own our truth, it can't be used against us. When we have secrets, people can use those secrets as power against us. In Hollywood, most publicists spend their time keeping their clients *in* the closet. I'm the guy you come to when you want to come out. And as your (admittedly self-appointed) publicist, I want you to consider this as the perfect time to come out with regard to whatever truth you've been holding in. It takes an enormous amount of emotional energy to keep a secret. And as we all know, the truth truly sets us free.

CHAPTER 19

THE PIÑATA SYNDROME AND HOW TO AVOID IT

In *Michael Clayton,* George Clooney plays an attorney who's a fixer. Asked to clean up a hideous mess his client has gotten into, Clooney says, "I'm not a miracle worker, I'm a janitor." In this chapter, we're going to talk about cleanup work, but on a very high level, of course.

The Piñata Syndrome means dealing with crises, self-inflicted or otherwise. Once you're in the public eye, it's almost inevitable that someone is going to want to take a poke at you, as if you were a piñata and not a person. "What's the point of building someone up," the media reasons, "if we can't knock them down?" Because there is virtually no distinction between the public and the private, it's likely that a matter you might deem private will spill over into the media. In this chapter, we're going to talk about how to handle crises so that your reputation, your career, and your sanity all remain intact.

We live in an era where haters can do their hating in public with just a few keystrokes on a computer, and they can upload their animosity to the Internet for all to see. Understanding how to cope with crises is a critically important aspect of creating and maintaining a public image. In my career, I've worked with countless celebrities, each of whom could have saved a busload of children from going over a cliff and they still would have been subject to criticism. The event was staged. They wasted gas or contributed to global warming by hitting the accelerator and keeping the bus on the narrow road. When people don't like you, they just plain don't like you, and they'll do everything they can to destroy you. It's my job to do everything I can to make sure that doesn't happen.

How do you avoid a crisis in the first place? The simplest advice is to live a clean life. As *Dr. 90210* reminded us in an earlier chapter, you want to act as if there's a camera on you all the time. In today's world more than ever, we do need to act as though anything we say or do could end up on the front page of the *New York Times* tomorrow, because that's more likely than ever to happen. In an era of citizen journalism, anyone with a cell phone equipped with a video camera, which is to say practically everyone in society, can suddenly be the next Zapruder, the man who chronicled John F. Kennedy's assassination, or George Holliday, the individual who videotaped the Rodney King beating. A man in Oklahoma calls himself the Video Vigilante and makes a solid six-figure income chasing prostitutes and their customers with his video camera and selling the footage to TV outlets (and posting it on the Web). Who knew you could find a prostitute in Oklahoma? A lot of people might call that progress. Indeed, lots of people are wandering around with video equipment much more sophisticated than is found in a cell phone, hoping to strike it rich.

The second piece of advice I can offer you is this: get your secrets out before others do. This was the focus of the previous chapter, coming out of the closet, and it's a great way to ensure that others don't have dirt on you, because you've already put the information into the public sphere. The third and best piece of advice that I can offer is this: prepare for a crisis before the crisis strikes. That way, you've done everything you need to do when trouble happens. The last thing you want to do when a crisis hits is to think about what your cleanup plan should be. Rudy Giuliani, while campaigning for president, spoke of the fact that New York City simply did not have a plan for what to do if two planes struck the World Trade Center. But New York had been subjected to terrorist attacks in the past, and Giuliani said the result of those strikes was an element of fear.

The smartest thing to do with fear, Giuliani told his audiences, was to turn it into preparation. Although New York did not have a specific plan for what actually happened on 9/11, it did have a plan for what happened if the hospitals were overwhelmed due to a terrorist attack. It did have a plan for what to do if the airports were shut down, or if public transportation could not be used. On 9/11, the city was able to craft a plan simply by stitching together the various crisis management plans it had created in the past. Thus Manhattan was not caught totally flat-footed when the unexpected attacks took place, and government and emergency services were able to respond effectively, for the most part, in the heat of the moment. The assumption to make in public life today is that a crisis can and will occur, and your job is to figure out in advance how best to handle it.

Who will speak for your company or organization? What are the phone numbers of the people in the media who will be your primary contacts? What are the lines of responsibility within your organization? What happens if the CEO or main spokesperson is tragically killed in a plane crash? When Armand Hammer, the CEO of Occidental Petroleum, passed away, the only individual authorized to speak for the company was the president of the company, and he wouldn't talk. So this extremely important company was in the awkward position of being unable to speak about the death of its founder. That's not great crisis management planning. Again, the time to think about these things is in advance of a crisis situation. It's just like the saying about buying life insurance: you're better off being a year early than an hour too late.

Let's assume that some things happen that cast you in a bad light—a disparaging newspaper article, a rumor on the Internet, or something else along these lines. The first thing to ask is this: Is this really a crisis? One of my mentors used to say that if no one is dead or seriously injured, then there is no crisis. I think that's a little harsh. If your property, reputation, or relationships are threatened, I consider that serious, and I consider that rising to the level of a crisis that must be handled. You want to ask yourself whether you have a real disaster on your hands, or just the potential for one. Someone threatening to sue is very different from someone actually going to court and filing papers. You have to ask yourself honestly whether you experienced a crisis . . . or just a bad day.

You also want to ask yourself whether there is true culpability in the situation. When the bridge in Minnesota collapsed, was it simply an accident, or was it heavy materials used for the refurbishing of the bridge that caused gussets to bow? In other words, is what happened bad luck or is it something more insidious? And if you are in crisis mode, are you handling the situation honestly? The toy companies, for example, wanted it both ways. They wanted to tell the world that they were doing everything they could to get the lead out of imported toys, but they wanted to continue to sell toys made overseas, because the profit margins were so much higher than those made domestically. So you've got to be prepared to tell the truth first to yourself before you can expect the rest of the world to believe you.

And then you've got to be able to keep things in perspective. *Business Week* was going to run a story on L.A. Gear back when I was running a new public relations company, and I was scared. I got a copy of the story faxed ahead of time, and the story was bad news for L.A. Gear, and by extension, for me. As soon as I saw that story, my heart sank. Before I knew it, I would be riding the Greyhound bus back to Flint, living on the streets, eating dog food the rest of my life. Okay, that might have been a little dramatic. I spoke to one of my mentors in the business, and he reminded me, "Howard, it's tennis shoes." The company survived the story, and so did my career.

Sometimes a crisis isn't a bad thing—it's something we can

use to our own advantage. That same company, L.A. Gear, created a TV commercial where it criticized its competitors by saying that "Everything else is hot air." The other major shoe companies leaned on the TV networks to say that the commercial was inappropriate because it was criticizing other people's brands. Perfect, I thought. I called CNN and told them about the controversy raging over the L.A. Gear commercial that the networks wouldn't run. CNN did a story, giving us a free airing of the commercial. You couldn't ask for much more than that.

This brings back to mind the concept of the noncontroversial controversy, which we discussed in an earlier chapter. When Illinois and Ft. Worth got into a spat over who had the better business climate, both sides won. When Rosie and Donald got into it, they both achieved their main desire in life, which is to see their names in the paper. How do you know you have a noncontroversial controversy on your hands? When there's no lasting damage and both parties benefit, that's exactly what you've got. Donald Trump owns the Miss California U.S.A. Pageant, and one fine day, one of the organizers of that pageant called him to give him the terrible news that they had awarded the crown to the wrong candidate. Trump was giddy with the news, because this would make it easier than ever to get his name into the paper that day. So a crisis, whether real or imagined, can be something that you can use to your benefit. If you're going to follow the noncontroversial controversy route to crisis management, just be sure that no one will be hurt when the story breaks.

Let's talk for a moment about how quickly you should respond when a disaster strikes. In today's Internet-driven world, crises can explode in mere seconds and can find their way around the world in the blink of an eye. One piece of information put on a blog or a single news report can explode into an international contretemps as never before. So it's very important, when responding to a situation like this, to take a beat. Pause before you wade in. Make sure that all the bad news is already out, and then take your best shot. Mel Gibson apologized too soon when he had his awkward situation with the California State Highway Patrol.

So did Floyd Landis, who was utterly and painfully unprepared for the media onslaught that followed the first news of his having failed a drug test during the 2006 Tour de France. If either of those individuals had taken the time to compose themselves before launching into a defense or an apology, they would have been much better served. If you don't wait until all the facts are out, you end up having to apologize over and over again, and that just ends up looking very unprofessional. An individual who did things the right way was Marion Jones. When she gave up her Olympic gold medals after having admitted to using performance enhancing drugs, she did so in a classy, dignified way. She clearly regretted her mistakes, and she walked away without the medals but with a great deal of respect for "owning" her mistake. By contrast, Barry Bonds continuously denies his steroid abuse, to the point where he became not only the poster child for baseball's so-called steroids era, but also may have brought down the entire investigation into performance enhancing drugs that left the sport in a state of deep embarrassment.

Sometimes speed can cause mistakes as happened to me when my client Isaiah Washington was let go from *Grey's Anatomy*. We had literally moments to respond to a barrage of media calls. Seeking a way to avoid hours of explanation, I believed a quote was the way to go. I chose a quote from the movie *Network*—"I'm mad as hell and I'm not going to take it anymore." I made a huge mistake.

While the quote was all about absurdity—which the situation certainly was—it didn't play well. People in the media focused on the anger and not the absurdity.

Even though Isaiah approved the quote, I own all responsibility for that bad decision. We discussed it later and he explained to me that we simply reinforced the stereotype of "the angry black man." He forgave me and continues with an exceptional career befitting the fine actor he is.

One time, I even ended up in the middle of a celebrity moment. I have represented Paula Abdul more than once in my career and known her for more than two decades since she first did a shoe line for L.A. Gear. I was asked to represent her for the last few weeks of *American Idol*. I respect Paula's ability to rise to the top in many professions, but frankly, we didn't see eye to eye PR-wise.

I'm working at my desk one afternoon and I get a call from a reporter at Page Six, the legendary *New York Post* gossip column. They wanted to know how I wanted to respond to some charges Paula had made on a tape about me. Well, I got to listen to the tape, and she said I called her "a crying, whining bitch." I didn't. I did tell her that if we could have a meeting or phone call where she didn't bust into tears our time might be more productive.

So I told Page Six, I don't want to get into this. And I hung up the phone. After calling a couple of people I respect for their advice, I called back and gave the official statement, "I'll stand by my reputation if she stands by hers."

My intent was not to trash Paula. I didn't believe she leaked the tape and probably felt very violated herself. She did not use the tape as a means to trash talk me further. She expressed dismay that her personal conversation was leaked to the media. Had she gone after me again, I would have defended myself, but felt no need to as she was handling it with some dignity.

It went viral and surprisingly wide. Oh, the drama.

After it was over I sent Paula a personal e-mail telling her that I knew she didn't leak the tape; that I wasn't mad at her; and that when I saw her next I would give her a hug and a kiss as was our custom. I did run into her a few months later and am happy to report that that's exactly what happened. Of course neither my staff nor the media knew about my e-mail and they all held their breaths and cameras when they realized the two of us were about to run into each other.

Think also about Senator Larry Craig, who was arrested for inappropriate behavior in an airport men's room. His on-again, off-again, now feisty, now contrite approach impressed no one. A smarter approach would have been for him to take a moment or two and compose himself and get some good advice. I would have had him make a statement that he was confronting these feelings, I would have sent him off to "gay rehab" for a couple of weeks, and then have him come out and make another statement—despite what I've learned, I still have homophobic feelings. His conservative constituency would have eaten it up like strawberry ice cream, and the whole thing would have blown over. Another person who did not handle a situation, with disastrous consequences, was Michael Vick. In our society, when you do something bad to animals, it's almost worse than if you murdered people. On the Friday after the events came to light, Vick denied them, and then the following Monday, not only did he accept responsibility but he told the world that he found religion over the weekend. I didn't buy it and I'm sure that you didn't, either. In short, just because *you* want the crisis to go away doesn't mean it will on your time frame, especially if you don't handle it right. You have to endure the process and make people believe you are redeemed. Redemption takes time. It's never instant.

How do you handle a real, live crisis? First, be honest. Be credible. Get ahead of the bad news by getting it all out there. Two days after the *Mitchell Report* came out, in which Senator George Mitchell exposed dozens of current and former Major League Baseball players as drug cheats, New York Yankees star Andy Pettitte made a statement that was perfect from a public relations standpoint. He admitted using HGH and said that he had only done it twice in his career, both times to recover from an injury and not to enhance his performance. He said that his HGH use represented just two days out of his entire career, that he had made a mistake, and that he was deeply contrite. America is a forgiving nation, and Pettitte did the right thing. He stepped up and apologized. No one could ask for more than that, and his career was unaffected. If, however, it turned out that Pettitte had actually used HGH on an ongoing basis, that initial statement would have been the worst possible thing he could have done.

Another rule to consider when crafting a response to a crisis is this: if someone has it on video, it's going to be a million times worse. Again, anyone with a cell phone can become an instant videographer and can reap a fortune from the various Internet Web sites that specialize in celebrity flogging. Not long ago, an actor whom I represent was accused of uttering a slur in public. Before we responded, I had to know whether someone had made a video of it. My client insisted they didn't, so we put out a denial.

Perhaps the classic case of someone whose career was undone by a video is the actor Michael Richards, famous for his role as Kramer on *Seinfeld* and infamous for his use of racial epithets in a comedy club appearance in Los Angeles. It would have been bad enough had no one videotaped his act. But the video, which was viewed endlessly on the Internet, sealed his fate. Richards made matters worse by making a statement with regard to "Afro-Americans," which is decidedly not a term that African-Americans use to describe themselves. As one African-American client told me, "Afro is a hairstyle, not a person." So Richards only dug his grave deeper when he sought to apologize. And it was very nice of Jerry Seinfeld to go on a talk show and stick up for his friend, but it made Richards look as though he was unwilling or unable to defend himself, that he had to send his big brother into action for him.

Sometimes, even PR-savvy individuals can make mistakes, including this humble author. At the time that the movie *Schindler's List* came out, a real estate client of mine was trying to sell a beautiful contemporary house in Los Angeles owned by a man named Schindler. On Friday, at my suggestion, we took out an ad in the *Hollywood Reporter* for the house under the instantly regrettable headline, "Schindler's Listing." What were we thinking? This was a very, very bad idea, and within hours, he and I were both receiving intense criticism and threats. The next day, the story ended up on the front page of the *L.A. Times* Calendar section. We humbly called Rabbi Marvin Hier of the Holocaust

Museum here in Los Angeles and explained that we were two nice Jewish boys who had displayed an appalling lack of judgment. Today, the story would have received much harsher treatment and would have lasted longer on the Internet, where anything negative simply gets more traction.

Another rule about crisis management is this classic piece of advice: don't get in fights with people who buy ink by the barrel. In other words, you may or may not be able to fight City Hall, but you certainly cannot fight the media. If the media does you wrong, you're either going to have to lump it or you'd better have equal or stronger media contacts on your side along with really solid evidence that you were right and, say, the *New York Times* was wrong. But good luck to you. It just doesn't pay to pick a fight with the media, which combines a long reach with an even longer institutional memory. If you get smeared, it may be the better part of valor just to let it go.

How do you handle true crises? The best advice might come from Gene Kelly in the classic movie *Singin' in the Rain*: "Dignity, always dignity." My client Monica Lewinsky went from being an unknown White House intern to perhaps the most famous person on the planet. Monica handled her unwanted place in the limelight with enormous dignity. She would be the first to acknowledge making a mistake, but no human being should be exposed to the level of wrath expressed against her and her family. It was disproportionately offensive. First, she was locked in a hotel room with ten or twelve government agents who were seeking to get a confession from her as to exactly what the nature of her relationship was with the president, when the reality was that the crime had been committed by the president against her. They even threatened to put her parents in jail, but Monica held her ground. This was a case of someone with presidential resources going up against a private citizen and trying to destroy her.

People don't realize that Monica Lewinsky, who became the subject of jokes across the country and across the world, could have cashed in on many millions after her ordeal. Everybody wanted the first TV interview, the first magazine interview, the first book, and she would have been set for life financially had she accepted those offers. She did not. Ultimately, she did accept a book deal, but she didn't make nearly as much as people thought, and she and her family had millions of dollars in legal fees to pay. When Bill Clinton finally apologized to her, her father mentioned to me how disappointed he was that Clinton had not apologized to her family as well. "He tore our family apart," her father said. "Monica's not the only victim here."

I leaked the story that the Lewinskys were not happy that no one had apologized to them, and within twenty-four hours, President Clinton apologized again, this time to the entire family. Was it a nice feeling to push those presidential buttons? You bet. More importantly, I have nothing but affection and respect for the way they stood together as a family. They chose dignity over dollars.

Once your crisis passes, and it invariably will, there comes a time for what I like to call the cathartic moment. This can be a warm, amusing moment that naturally arises when the heat has died down, when the courtroom proceedings are over, when the jail term has ended, when we can all look back and laugh. Hugh Grant epitomized the cathartic moment when he went on Jay Leno asking the question "What was I thinking?" after having been arrested for soliciting a prostitute on Sunset Boulevard. Winona Ryder, by contrast, came to her cathartic moment too soon. You might recall that she wore a "Free Winona" T-shirt while her case was still going on, and while the judge was scrutinizing every aspect of her behavior to determine how best to resolve the case. That wasn't the brightest of moves in my opinion.

For Monica Lewinsky, her cathartic moment came with an appearance on *Saturday Night Live*. I called my old friend the late Hollywood legend Bernie Brillstein, who represented Lorne Michaels, the producer of *Saturday Night Live*. "Bernie, I'm working with Monica Lewinsky, and we think it's time to have our moment. I think she ought to go on *Saturday Night Live*. Do you think Lorne would be interested?"

"I think he might be interested," Bernie allowed with a chuckle, and within ten minutes, Lorne called me back to set a date for Monica's appearance a few weeks hence. Michaels is the hero of this story. He acted with enormous integrity and told Monica that any jokes she wanted cut would be cut. We got to see the script in advance and we in fact did take some things out that were either disrespectful to Monica or the president. All in all, it was a good experience for Monica and it began the process of reestablishing her identity as a decent person, all because of the integrity of Lorne Michaels.

In the years preceding the writing of this book, my role as publicist for major celebrities placed me in crisis management mode on many occasions. There are many things I cannot talk about, because the clients were able to resolve a court issue quietly, and without fanfare, or went off to rehab without a train of paparazzi following them in Humvees and helicopters. But there are a few I can talk about, and I do think they offer intriguing lessons about right and wrong ways to handle crises. The legendary sportscaster Jim Lampley, a friend for more than twenty years, was wrongfully accused of acting abusively in a relationship. I didn't believe it when I heard it, and against his attorney's advice, we promptly put out a denial. It turned out that the entire matter was spurious, Jim kept his job, and we won both in the courts of law and public opinion. If you are in the right, there's nothing wrong with saying so, quickly and firmly.

And then there's the case of Naomi Campbell. Let's just say that her cell phone accidentally struck her housekeeper in the head. How did that happen? Well, she's very tall, and she does have long legs, and maybe she tripped on her supermodel heels? Whatever. Well, Naomi was sentenced to community service, but how does a diva go to court for something like that? A true diva takes along a legendary fashion photographer, Steven Klein, to capture the moments. The photographs of Naomi ended up in a fantastic photo spread in *W*, the glossy Fairchild fashion magazine. All I can say is, you go, girl. Incidentally, one of the photos taken was of Naomi on my arm leaving the courthouse. It was a black-and-white photograph, and friends said it looked like a still from a *Perry Mason* episode. It just shows how times have changed. Half a century ago, if you were leaving the courthouse, you left on the arm of your attorney. Today, it's your publicist.

We talked at length about John Amaechi, the basketball player who came out and whose story became much bigger than anyone might have imagined. During the course of those events, basketball star Tim Hardaway made some homophobic remarks about Amaechi. We have a term for this in public relations. We call it . . . a gift. In sports terms, you could describe it as "an assist by Tim Hardaway at the buzzer." Hardaway's inappropriate remarks took a big story and shoved it into the stratosphere. Amaechi was able to say, "The NBA claims there is no homophobia—but I told you so." Final score? For Amaechi, the *New York Times* best-seller, the high income, and the speaking engagements. For Hardaway? He lost his association with the NBA, changed the name of his car wash, and had to apologize. Intriguingly, the stigma moved from the gay athlete to the homophobic athlete. The lesson: if someone hands you a gift, use it.

Another client of mine was the young, beautiful Cuban fiancée of race car driver Helio Castroneves, who was victorious on *Dancing with the Stars*. The question that kept arising during his appearances on that show was this: Where's your fiancée? In reality, the engagement was over, but he just did not want to say so. His fiancée got tired of the questions from her friends and family, who wanted to know why Helio was not telling the truth. I crafted an item for TMZ.com, after he had done all of his media like *Good Morning America* and *Regis and Kelly*, so as not to interfere with his moment in the sun. My statement said that the two were no longer engaged, and that she would not talk to media unless it was necessary to clarify misstatements in order to defend her reputation, and that the right contact person was me, not her.

My desire was to get the message out without having to place her in a media spotlight she did not desire. I called the publicist on *Dancing with the Stars*, whom I knew from other shows we had worked on together in the past, and I told her that we just wanted to get the statement out. We didn't want to go to war, but if Helio had any mean things to say about her, we certainly would. Ten minutes later, *she* released a statement to People.com saying that Helio does confirm that the engagement is over and hoped that everyone would respect the privacy of both individuals. In my world, that's a victory. We got the result we wanted—my client had the opportunity to get out of the media spotlight, and Helio was no longer spinning the concept that he was still engaged to her.

This might sound like a lot of Hollywood back story, but the lesson for anyone caught in the public eye is that it's tough to disengage with the media by telling them that you're disengaging. The media is just too hungry a beast, and it especially wants what it cannot have. If you want to lie low, then lie low. Pay someone else to tell the media you're lying low, because if you make a statement to that effect, the media will never believe you.

Finally, the good news is that in a society like ours, practically anything can be forgiven. Martha Stewart is more successful today than ever. Jason Giambi, the New York Yankees baseball star, apologized for taking performance enhancing drugs without ever actually mentioning performance enhancing drugs, and the fans have embraced him fully. A nude photo of Vanessa Hudgens, the star of Disney's *High School Musical*, was widely distributed on the Internet. She came out and apologized, and said that she had made a mistake when she was younger. The proof of her forgiveness is the fact that Disney cast her in *High School Musical 3*. (And will probably cast her in *High School Musical 146*, when that one comes out too.)

The point of all this is to say that the best way to avoid crises is to keep your nose clean. But let's deal in reality. We all make mistakes, we all stumble from time to time, and we all need forgiveness and redemption. If you handle a crisis situation correctly—take a moment to get all of your facts straight, stay ahead of the bad news by releasing all of it instead of waiting for the media to hit you while you're down, and apologize appropriately and sincerely, the world will forgive you. Your career will continue, and the sun will rise in the morning—and isn't that the best news of all?

Let's keep things in perspective. Your career can shrug off a few mistakes. What you can't afford is to keep the good things you do a secret. Now you know everything I know about getting your light out from under the bushel so that it—and you—can shine.

THE TEN COMMANDMENTS OF PR

created these "commandments" because the rules have changed. People still believe that any press is good press, that getting press is always a good thing...and as we've seen, it's not. So here are the new rules of the road.

1. All press is not good press. And the corollary is: just because you can get press doesn't mean you should get press. Just ask Heather Mills or Michael Jackson.

2. Perception is reality. PR no longer stands for public relations—as we've discussed, it stands for perception and reality. I spoke to a client recently accused of inappropriate behavior. "It's not true." he exclaimed. "It doesn't matter," I told him. "If it gets out there, it will be perceived as true, and that's all that matters."

3. Create a brand. That's what former president George H. W. Bush called "the vision thing." Your PR must work toward a purpose. Smart celebrities are not on TV or in the media unless they have something to sell or a message to shape. It's all about building your personal brand. A brand is broad-based—it's not just one thing. It's your career, your personal life, your look . . . the whole gestalt, if you will.

4. *The truth seeks its own level . . . eventually.* If you're attacked with an untruth, you can take comfort in the fact that the truth ultimately will surface. Conversely, if you tell a lie, you're planting your own landmine. You may forget about it until later, but it will always be there. This also brings to mind the "iceberg theory"—if you see a few problems, you can count on the fact that there are many more under the surface. When a president leaves office, there's always a rush to write "tell-all" books about what really happened behind the scenes. In Hollywood, when someone reaches a level of stardom, people write tell-all books about them too. These books are fairly accurate. The truth, ugly or not, inevitably surfaces . . . eventually.

5. *Energize your base.* Identify your core supporters . . . and never forget them. Oprah would never forget the African-American community. Eva Longoria will never forget her Latino base. These are the people who were with you at first, who support you most strongly, and who will most ardently convey your message to others. A forgotten base can be like a jilted lover. Need I say more?

6. *The media will not wait for you.* And in today's media world, speed trumps accuracy. There are dozens of effects of PR technology on our world, and the very nature of PR has changed. That lightning won't go back in any bottle. The metabolism of the media has only sped up over the years. If you don't deal with the media in the new millennium, you simply won't be a part of the new millennium. On the information highway, you'll be roadkill.

7. *There is no wall between public and private.* From cameraphones to blogs, from valet parkers to bouncers, from ER nurses to waiters, what they see is what the world gets. Welcome to the fishbowl. Some have called fame a "bitch goddess." That statement is more true than ever. The bad news about being in the public eye is that the public eye never blinks, never needs Visine, looks good with or without makeup, and it's now watching *you.*

8. *The medium is still the message.* A story is only as credible as the newspaper, magazine, TV show, or blog that carries it. I have a celebrity client involved in an unattractive divorce. The story was leaked to the *National Enquirer.* The other side accused us of leaking it. I responded, "If we leaked it somewhere, it wouldn't be to the *National Enquirer.*" If I leak a story, it's to a credible media outlet, because otherwise, I damage the story's credibility.

9. *They're only building you up to knock you down.* The media charges for its services on the back end—which means that the cost of putting you on a pedestal is that the media will always want to knock you off it. Accusations are inevitably front page news; final verdicts, especially in your favor, only rate a couple of paragraphs on an inside page. Remember that Richard Jewell, the alleged Atlanta Olympics bomber, died at age forty-five, no doubt in large measure due to the false accusations against him. Everyone remembers the charges; few know that he was exonerated.

10. *Everyone has a second act.* One of the most beautiful aspects of our Judeo-Christian culture is the concept of forgiveness. Even if you're an atheist or an agnostic, I contend that forgiveness is noble. By definition, human beings are flawed. Ever heard of the phrase "human error"? The good news is that the vast majority of people learn from their mistakes. They not only try to become better themselves, but the smart ones use their mistakes to help others become better too . . . and that makes all of us better. In America, the land of second chances, down is decidedly not out.

AFTERWORD

☆ *BY HARVEY LEVIN, CREATOR AND EXECUTIVE PRODUCER, TMZ*

In the world of celebrity, the universe has changed over the last five years. In the old days (the '90s), secrets could be kept secrets. Lies could be disseminated as truth. False images often turned into reality.

The fact is, publicists had a stranglehold on traditional media. They knew the media operated out of fear—a weakness that was simple to exploit. Publicists could bludgeon producers of traditional entertainment TV shows and editors of newspapers and magazines into running what they wanted, or else. If a producer dared air an unflattering story about a star, forget ever getting on the red carpet for the actor's next premiere.

When I created *Celebrity Justice,* a TV show that was in some ways the precursor to TMZ, my premise was to eliminate the fear and operate out of fairness. Who cares if a big actor won't do an interview with us? If we had a story that was fair and accurate, whether it was flattering or not, our MO was to call the publicist for comment, not permission.

Within a few years, the game changed and many publicists didn't know how to deal with it. The old tricks no longer worked, at least with us, though a number of publicists persisted in vain.

Howard Bragman was one of the first publicists to notice the seismic change and respond accordingly. I remember dealing with Howard and telling him how we had a story that wasn't particularly flattering but that we would be fair and publish his client's point of view on the matter—in other words, we would give him the best bad story he could get. I argued that the story was going to get out anyway, and if he just rolled the dice and watched someone do a skewed, inaccurate account, he would end up doing damage control for months. As strange as that seems, it's a rather high concept that a lot of publicists had trouble with. Howard got it immediately.

It used to be that publicists could create an image for clients and a frightened media would gladly play along, deceiving the public with images and content that bore no relationship to reality. Fact is, being a bully is much easier than being a craftsman, and the publicist world was populated with too many of the former.

There's no doubt—celebrity news is being covered differently, not just on the Internet but in traditional media. It's not about digging up dirt; it's about portraying reality. It's not about good stories and bad stories; it's about truthful stories. The public isn't buying false images like they used to, and besides, all the phoniness is boring compared to what's real. So the question is, with the massive changes in the way celebrities are covered, have publicists responded? Many of them have, but some—not surprisingly, some of the ones who were the most powerful—have been slow to adapt.

Howard has figured it out. A bad story is almost never a career ender: the Paris Hilton sex tape made her a star; Britney Spears can rise again with a good CD. The trick to publicity is accepting what you can't change and looking at each story as a snapshot and not the entire movie.

In my business, I deal with scores of people behind the scenes—publicists, lawyers, family, and friends of celebs. There are people I trust and people I don't. If a publicist lies to me or feigns ignorance, it's not something I forget. The next time they call, I'm definitely suspicious and it's going to be much harder for them to use me. Yes, I said "use me." Every journalist is used by sources. Why else would they be talking to you? They have an agenda and we have a duty to report what's fair and accurate. The two are not mutually exclusive. But I'm much more receptive to straight shooters than bullshitters.

The subtle thread that runs throughout this book is that publicists can be effective in managing news about their clients as well as how their clients deal with the media. In this world, a celebrity's art just isn't enough. Sad, perhaps, but undeniably true.

ACKNOWLEDGMENTS

No one does this alone. I am humbly indebted to the many, many people who made this book a reality.

First, to my business partners—past and present—what a journey it's been. Thanks Mike, Brad, Chris, Susan, and Helene at BNC. And to Bill, Ryan, Gabe, Lisa, and Pete at Fifteen Minutes—we're still having fun.

To all my employees, current and past: I get so much credit and you do so much of the work. It does not go unnoticed and I am eternally grateful to each of you.

To my nephew Adam, who is also my assistant, who cleans up a lot of my messes.

Over the years I have had the privilege of representing hundreds of people, companies, and causes. Thank you for your trust and support.

My parents, Myrna and Leonard, and my brother, Alan, gave me the love, support, and foundation to achieve my dreams.

My grandmother Leah Wolin taught me about giving back, and my grandfather David Wolin taught me about living richly.

My hundreds of students at USC's Annenberg School proved

the adage that the teacher learns more than the students. Thanks for that.

My friends in the media need to know that even when they said no, I still appreciated their ability to listen.

The gang at Showbiz Tonight gets my love and gratitude. A.J., Brooke, Dave, Albert, Mara, Brittany, and Toya—you rock.

Larry King, Wendy, and Ryan—thanks for letting me sit in that iconic chair.

Leeza, Dana, and Vincent—thanks for recognizing that I have a face for radio.

To Harvey Levin, even when I don't like what's in the column.

To my friend David Ehrenstein, who helped me develop the original Ten Commandments of PR.

Thanks to David Kessler, Jaron Lowenstein, Owen Moogan, Eric Ober, and Amy Pfister for reviewing early drafts of the book and offering great suggestions.

Thanks to Miriam Eichler Rivas and Ross Johnson, who went along for part of this journey.

Michael Levin, you took me from crayons to perfume and completed the journey with me. I literally couldn't have done it without you.

Matthew Guma—thanks for believing in me and my idea.

And finally, to Adrian Zackheim, who embodies the finest qualities of a book editor. You, Courtney, Allison, and your team are magnificent.

INDEX